P9-CFM-769

making more of small spaces

making more of
small spaces

by Stephen Crafti

Published in Australia in 2003 by
The Images Publishing Group Pty Ltd
ACN 89 059 734 431
6 Bastow Place, Mulgrave, Victoria 3170, Australia
Telephone (61 3) 9561 5544 Facsimile (61 3) 9561 4860
Email: books@images.com.au
Website: www.imagespublishinggroup.com

Copyright © The Images Publishing Group Pty Ltd 2003
The Images Publishing Group Reference Number: 525

All rights reserved. Apart from any fair dealing for the purpose of private
study, research, criticism or review as permitted under the Copyright Act,
no part of this publication may be reproduced, stored in a retrieval system
or transmitted in any form by any means, electronic, mechanical,
photocopying, recording or otherwise, without the written
permission of the publisher.

National Library of Australia
Cataloguing-in-Publication Data

Crafti, Stephen, 1959- .
Making More of Small Spaces.

ISBN 1 920744 25 8.

1. Space (Architecture). 2. Interior Architecture.
3. Small Houses. 4. Room Layout (Dwellings). I. Title.

747.8831

Film by Mission Productions Limited
Printed by Everbest Printing Co. Ltd. in Hong Kong/China

IMAGES has included on its website a page for special notices
in relation to this and our other publications. It includes updates
in relation to the information printed in our books. Please visit
this site: www.imagespublishinggroup.com

Contents

Introduction

As vacant land becomes scarce, particularly in inner cities, architects are becoming more inventive in designing small spaces. Small footprints require large impressions. The building's envelope is stretched to its maximum.

With sites often measuring no more than 5 metres in width, and 15 to 20 metres in depth, it has become crucial to include a third level in any development. And instead of a backyard, the roof terrace is often the solution to creating outdoor space. With increased light and city views afforded from the top levels, the living and entertaining areas are often designed at the higher levels of the house, adjacent to these roof terraces.

While the sites are small, the ideas in each of these 'pockets' are substantial. Courtyards replace gardens, laundries and powder rooms are tucked into tight alcoves, and kitchen appliances disappear from view, concealed behind cupboards. Even the problem of finding space for an extra bedroom can be solved, with one architect creating a plinth at the top of the stairs for the new bed. In another instance, when a second bedroom is only required for guests, an entire wall can be shifted to create the space. Clearly the success of these spaces is their flexibility and ingenuity in making the one space perform several functions. A kitchen may be a kitchen between certain hours and then take the form of a living area for the remainder of the day.

Many of the homes featured in this book were built at the turn of the century. Quaint when they were built and appropriate for a certain way of living (generally indoors and away from sunlight). A shotgun corridor

by Stephen Crafti

down one side of the house appeared in many of these homes. But with a move away from formal living and towards using the outdoor terrace as another room, these homes required substantial reworking, and in most cases, opening up entirely. While some of the original features in these homes have been retained, there is a new contemporary imprint stamped on each design.

Walls have been removed from many of the old homes to create larger and more fluid spaces. And even when there are doors, many are sliding. When they are pulled right back, the spaces can borrow from an adjoining passage. But while some architects eliminate as many walls as possible, there are those that incorporate the corridor into their designs, creating a journey as one moves through the spaces.

With small spaces, light is one of the most crucial factors. Certainly many of the white walls in these homes brighten the interiors. But other means are used to bring light to these spaces, making them feel considerably larger. A pond in one courtyard was seen as a way of spreading light and the water's reflection into a living area. Other designs rely on using overhead skylights and glass in numerous forms, from clear to frosted and sandblasted.

As the price of land increases in cities worldwide and the structure of households change, the idea of living in a small space has become accepted. However, it is only once past the front door that many of these heroic designs can fully be appreciated. This book allows us to go beyond the front door and look at many substantial architectural designs, irrespective of their size.

Projects

Reworking the Spaces

This townhouse was only a few years old before being completely redesigned. Originally a redbrick speculative project home, the architects were called in to completely rework the design.

While the top two levels, consisting of bedrooms, were modified, the ground floor was fully reworked by Inarc Architects. In the original design there was an internal light well that connected the top two levels. 'It was meant to be an outdoor terrace, but it was completely enclosed (except at the roof). It was full of leaves and barely anything grew,' says architect Reno Rizzo.

The light well was used to contain the stairs between the top two levels, and a third staircase was designed to link these stairs to the ground level. The ground floor was gutted and, unlike most renovations where the original footprint is enlarged, the new design decreased the floor space by approximately 10 percent. 'We wanted to increase the size of the garden,' says Rizzo, who incorporated a shallow reflective pool. 'The pool adds depth to the internal spaces. There's an illusion of space,' he says.

In the original design, the kitchen was at the back of the house and the formal sitting area was at the front. But with the morning light maximised at the front of the house, the layout was reconfigured with the two functions exchanging positions. Instead of a series of rooms, the architects designed one continuous vista to the backyard. And instead of walls defining each space, Inarc used alternative methods. A glass balustrade/wall divides the dining room from the living room on the half-level below. In between the dining room and the kitchen, Inarc designed three separate storage units, of American walnut. As Rizzo says, 'They separate the spaces, but they still allow visual contact to the other areas of the house.'

Inarc Architects Pty Ltd   Photography by Peter Clarke

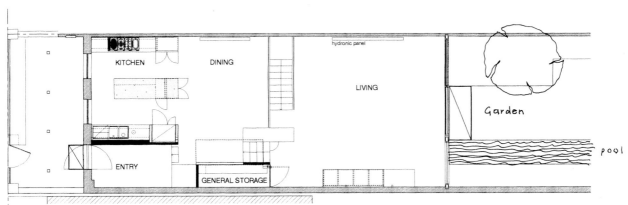

KITCHEN

DINING

hydronic panel

LIVING

Garden

pool

ENTRY

GENERAL STORAGE

Providing an Alternative

The owners of this townhouse wanted to stay in the area. They were living in a 1920s house and couldn't decide whether to renovate or move into something smaller. The solution was to pull down the old house and build two new townhouses on the site, one to live in, the other to sell.

As the site is relatively compact, measuring 15 metres in width, by 37 metres in depth, car access to the rear unit is via a rear laneway. However, there was sufficient room across the site to provide a walkway from the street to the rear unit.

Designed by Provan Burdett Architects, the two townhouses are each approximately 150 square metres in size, but both have their own configurations. The rear townhouse was designed for the owners. The brief to the architects was simple. 'They were looking towards retirement and wanted something that was low maintenance. They also wanted the bedroom and living room on the ground level,' says architect David Burdett. A small study and guest bedroom were then designed for the second level.

To maximise an important component of the brief, 'light', Provan Burdett designed one large kitchen, dining and living space. The one space is orientated to a light-filled courtyard garden by full-length glass window-walls. The link to the garden is strengthened by means of two large glass pivotal doors. 'We designed an outdoor canopy to create a third option for our clients. When the doors are left open, the outdoor space can function as another room,' says Burdett.

The owners of this townhouse had a similar arrangement of rooms in their previous 1920s house. But in this case there are no walls. The three areas (kitchen, dining and living) are defined by furniture rather than walls. And to further define the spaces, the architects framed the kitchen and living spaces at either end with 2.5-metre bulkheads. As a result, the ceiling height at the centre of the space is notably higher (3.6 metres as opposed to 2.7 metres at either end).

'When you average the two ceiling heights, it feels considerably larger. There's a sense of volume with the height variations,' he adds. The main staircase, with its open treads, also appears significantly larger than those of many period homes with steep and enclosed staircases. Placed between full-length windows, the view from this staircase is towards the garden on either side. As Burdett says, 'You're not conscious of being in a relatively small space.'

Provan Burdett Pty Ltd   Photography by Derek Swalwell

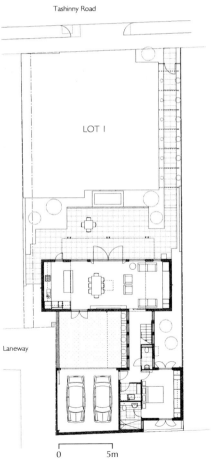

Tashinny Road

LOT 1

Laneway

0   5m

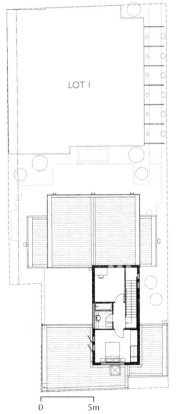

LOT 1

0   5m

Flexible Spaces

This city apartment was originally an office. 'It was a rabbit warren of partitions,' says architect Chris Idle, who renovated the apartment with his partner, architect Megan Harrison, for their own home. The apartment is below ground level but draws its light from the building's light well. And with 17 metres of floor-to-ceiling glass windows across one entire wall, the apartment is exceptionally light.

The apartment has two bedrooms, but one of the bedrooms has a large sliding door that can be pulled right back to create extra space in the entrance/passageway. The same bedroom also has a moveable wall (on casters). Facing the bedroom, the wall was designed with built-in wardrobes. The other side of the moveable wall contains the television set and a drawer for storage. 'This wall can be entirely removed and pushed back against another wall if extra space is required in the living area,' says architect Chris Idle. The spaces had to be flexible, as the apartment is less than 100 square metres in size.

The kitchen bench was also designed for flexibility. Made of solid plywood and white plastic laminate, the kitchen bench features a slot for the table to manoeuvre. 'It can be left to stand in the dining area in its full length (2.4 metres). Alternatively it can be moved into kitchen space and be shortened to half its size.' It then provides extra bench space in the kitchen. The study area was also designed to be flexible. Positioned along the main passage, a 5-metre hoop pine plywood desk can be used to work on or as a display area for objects.

Unlike many other apartments, where the entire space is seen immediately from the front door, Idle and Harrison tried to conceal the main living space from the entrance. This was achieved by locating the laundry within laminated cupboards, expressed as a cube within the space. 'It creates a barrier to the main vista and allowed us to set up a journey, however small it is,' says Idle.

Neil + Idle Architects Pty Ltd
in Association with Megan Harrison Architect

Photography by Megan Harrison

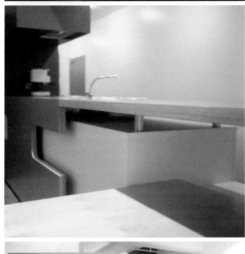

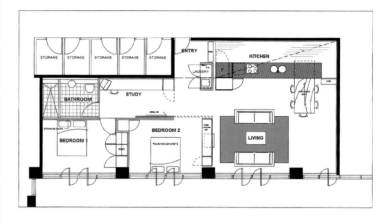

A Georgian Townhouse

This Georgian townhouse originally consisted of four rooms, two downstairs and two above. There was also a small kitchen and bathroom that had been tacked onto the house in more recent years. When the owners decided to extend their family, they decided to extend the house simultaneously.

The owners and the architect had lived in Tokyo for several years. Both were impressed with the way the Japanese approach small spaces and their ability to 'borrow' from their gardens. 'I was used to living behind shoji screens and making do with the small spaces I was living in,' says architect Grant Amon.

Amon retained the original four rooms in the house, but removed the bathroom and kitchen that had been added later. The wall to the second downstairs room was also removed and fully opened to the passage. What was previously a dining room became an informal sitting area. The original steep staircase, leading from the passage, was relocated to the sitting area and replaced with more gentle rises to the level above. Amon also designed a new bathroom with a blue and white glass screen in a checkerboard design. 'I had similar doors in my apartment in Tokyo. At night the light in the bathroom sheds a wonderful glow into the living areas. During the day, there's all the natural light to rely on,' says the owner.

In the rear yard, the old garage was removed and a new one designed. The new building also includes an upstairs office that can be used as a bedroom if guests decide to stay for the night. Made of cedar and corrugated steel, the building creates a protective wall to shield the courtyard from the harsher sunlight.

Mindful of the 2-metre slope on the site (measuring only 5 metres by 38 metres in depth), Amon devised a slate-covered platform outside the meals area to create a link to the garden. The architect was also careful not to create an extension with a long 'gun-barrel' corridor to one side of the house. Instead, a number of angles appear from the corridor, including the main downstairs bathroom with its checkerboard glass doors. Courtyards were used where possible too, in order to allow each space to breathe. As Amon says, 'The Georgian style is quite simple. I wanted to retain the same simple lines in the new work.'

This house first appeared in Domain, *The Age* newspaper, 25 June 2003.

Grant Amon Architect   Photography by Earl Carter and by Richard Briglia

A Slither of a Site

This Victorian worker's cottage originally only consisted of two main rooms, with a kitchen and bathroom tacked on. Inadequate for contemporary living, the owner was keen to update the house.

Located on a small site, 4 metres wide by 27 metres deep, the new design was also restricted by heritage controls in this inner-city location. In a row of eight identical houses that share one continuous roof, the architects were required to retain the first two rooms of this single-storey cottage. 'We also had to set the new work back 10 metres from the street. The new design wasn't permitted to be seen by those passing by,' says architect Jennifer Hocking of the practice Burne Hocking Weimar Architects, who renovated and extended the cottage.

A double-storey extension was added to the rear of the cottage, and includes a new kitchen, bathroom and living room. A new bedroom and roof deck were designed on the first floor. While the architects could have maximised the entire width of the site for the extension, they chose to set the building back 1 metre, creating a building width of only 3 metres. 'Our client valued light over the physical space. The additional light increases the feeling of space,' says Hocking. The angled glazed wall that runs along the bathroom, kitchen and living space helps to reduce the towering sensation of the two-storey extension over such a small site.

The wall of the extension is made of stained plywood cladding. The material creates a tactile and warm ambience from the pocket-sized garden. 'It's only a small garden, but it acts as another room. We didn't want the owner to feel as though she was pressed against a wall every time she used the garden,' says Hocking.

While the size of the site may have discouraged other architects, Burne Hocking Weimar embraced the many constraints. As Hocking says, 'You need to look at the positive qualities of the site and work with what you have.'

Burne Hocking Weimar Architects

Photography by Naomi Kumar

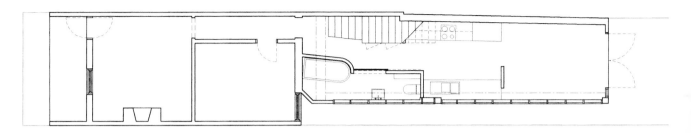

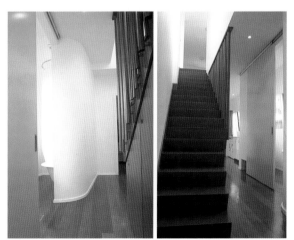

Maximising the Site

Designed by architect Peter Woolard as his home/office, this 13-square-metre house maximises the site, measuring 9 by 27 metres. It was not only the dimensions that inhibited the design. Situated on a main road, the site is bordered by garages from a set of units built in the 1960s. Heritage controls in the area also influenced the design in terms of setbacks, height and materials used. 'Sometimes you can turn restraints into positives,' says Woolard, who used materials for the house like those found in the streetscape. The architect also included in the design a 5-metre-high blade wall to increase privacy. The angled blade wall expanded the home's footprint on the site too.

The angled corrugated steel ceiling in the living and dining areas also increases the vertical space in the house. To ensure privacy from the existing units, Woolard used the wet areas as a buffer zone. The kitchen, laundry, bathroom and the ensuite to the main bedroom upstairs, all share the same wing. 'The area creates an acoustic and visual buffer. It's also economical to have all the plumbing in the one area,' he says.

The all-white laminate kitchen appears as one continuous wall. The workings such as the fridge, microwave and pantry are concealed behind cupboards. The only visible element in the kitchen is the stainless-steel oven and stove. 'When spaces are small, you really need to reduce things to the essentials,' says Woolard.

Split concrete blocks not only create a feature wall in the living area, but also act as divisions between the public and private areas. The concrete blocks are also used as an anchoring device. 'The other materials such as the plywood and glass are lighter and more skeletal,' says Woolard, who maximised the use of steel in the house for its strength and lightness too.

And though Woolard was hemmed in from all sides, he was still able to create a tranquil vista in the form of a Japanese-style garden. With the sound of cascading water in the background, the tight urban context is easily ignored.

This house first appeared in Domain, *The Age* newspaper, 16 October 2002.

Studio 101 Architects   Photography by Trevor Mein

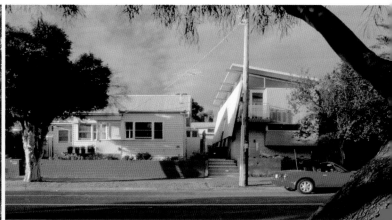

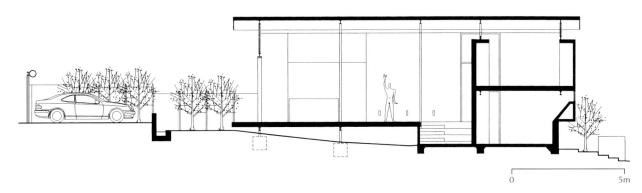

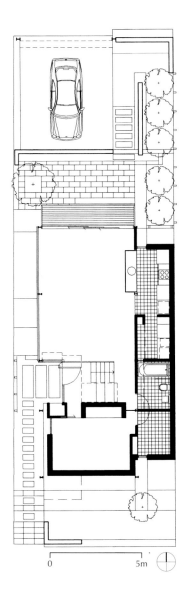

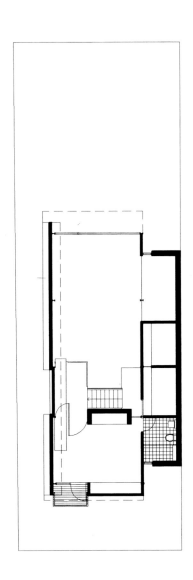

0   5m

A Former Chocolate Factory

This warehouse was previously used as a chocolate factory. It was divided into shells and sold off for residential development. 'We basically inherited four walls and a roof,' says architect Des Holmes. While the footprint on the ground was less than 80 square metres, the vertical spaces were considerably more generous. This allowed Holmes to conceive three levels in the design.

The ground floor, with its curvaceous wall, leads to the main bedroom and ensuite. There is also a study on the ground level, complete with a large sliding door. It can either be used as an office or bedroom. On the second level are the kitchen, living and dining areas. And on the third, is a small mezzanine bedroom, tucked into the rafters. Holmes was even able to provide a rooftop deck. 'My clients were keen to have some outdoor space. It wasn't possible on the ground level but they can climb the stairs and look out over the rooftops towards the city.'

One of the main problems with the original warehouse shell was the lack of natural light. To compensate, Holmes drew light through the space via an open-treaded timber staircase and steel-rigged balustrades. 'The stairs become a more translucent element in the space. The galley-style kitchen also suffered from limited natural light. While Holmes was unable to draw the natural light into this space, he compensated with the use of reflective materials such as colour-backed colour for the kitchen's splashbacks. 'The other constraint was the structural beams in the kitchen. We had to work around these,' says Holmes.

While the natural light is restricted, the available light is able to permeate the various levels in the warehouse. As one climbs the staircase, the impression is of an expanding space. As Holmes says, 'Your eye is being continually lead to the next level. You're not conscious of the four surrounding walls.'

Des Holmes Architects Pty Ltd

Photography by David Paul

A Different Approach

The choice in housing is often between the house on a quarter-acre block or the high-rise apartment. However, Jan + Manton Design Architecture devised their own alternative. 'We were thinking of a couple who want to live close to the city and they might have family or guests who regularly stay over,' says architect Chris Manton of Jan + Manton Design Architecture, who designed these three townhouses.

The irregular-shaped site benefited from a wide laneway on one side. 'The laneway becomes a secondary street. It enabled us to create separate and secluded entrances for the townhouses (two of which face the lane, the other fronting the street),' says Manton.

The design of the three-level townhouses was influenced by many of the post-war flats and 1920s detached homes in the street. The skillion-shaped roofs, the concrete stucco walls and the rhythmic pattern of neighbouring balconies, helped to shape the design. More contemporary materials included galvanised steel and cedar frames to create privacy, together with zinc panels to add texture to the building.

Unlike most medium-density housing, the three townhouses have their own configurations. The front townhouse, for example, has two rooms on the ground floor and a large bathroom and laundry. Designed to be flexible, the owners use one of the rooms for television, the other as a guest bedroom. 'Every room is different. It's not the traditional rectangular format found in most townhouses,' says one of the owners who lives in the front townhouse.

On the middle level, the open-plan kitchen, living and dining area is framed with generous balconies. And with relatively high ceilings (3 metres), the owners feel as though they are living in a house, rather than a unit. 'The amount of light we receive also makes it feel more spacious,' says the owner, who particularly enjoys the space and privacy of the bedroom and retreat located on the third level.

Jan + Manton Design Architecture   Photography by Tony Miller

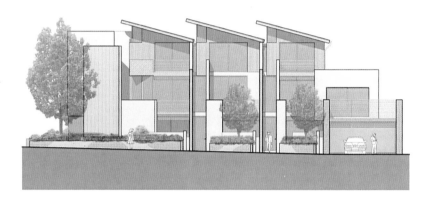

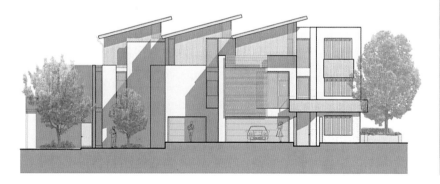

A Studio Apartment

This city warehouse was originally used to manufacture clothing. When purchased by the developers, the 1920s brick three-storey building contained many of its original features such as Baltic pine floors. The building also had loft ceilings, up to 3.6 metres in places.

Recently, the warehouse was converted into several apartments by Neometro Architects, ranging from small studios (60 square metres) to two-storey apartments (approximately 118 square metres). The original tin roof was removed and a concrete slab poured to accommodate the larger apartments. To separate the new work from the original building, the architects used titanium zinc rib sheeting for the new façade. 'This material is often used for traditional mansard roofs in Europe,' says architect Clare McAllister of Neometro.

A one-bedroom studio apartment, located on a corner of the second floor, overlooks two narrow laneways. Fortunately, while the views were restricted, the light was generous as a result of the large windows.

Consisting of a bedroom, a dining area and kitchen, a living area and a bathroom, this apartment was designed primarily for one person. The spaces were deliberately left as open as possible. The bedroom, for example, has a sliding door that can be pulled right back to allow the space to be shared with the dining area. 'You only need to close the bedroom doors if guests come over, or to conceal any clutter,' says McAllister. 'The only enclosed space is the bathroom,' she adds.

While the apartment is small, it benefits from generous ceiling heights. 'We really wanted to keep the space open and create that warehouse feel,' says Barry Ludlow of Neometro. Even the services, such as the pipes, are left exposed against the concrete ceiling. The pipes add a decorative element to the space. To reduce the space required for services such as plumbing, Neometro designed the bathroom adjacent to the kitchen. And storage, which is a common problem in small spaces, was tucked into the kitchen wall.

This studio apartment is small. But the architects have not compromised on quality and comfort in the space provided.

Neometro Architects   Photography by Peter Clarke

Seamless Design

Once a landmark office building, this building was converted into apartments a number of years ago. Originally designed by Demaine Russell Trundle Armstrong and Orton in the early 1960s, its curved façade creates a sense of elegance on the city's edge.

Unfortunately, the same elegance was not maintained in one two-bedroom, 120-square-metre apartment. While the views of the city skyline remained sharp, the interior became tired and faded. 'The kitchen was a combination of beige Imperite cupboards and pink granite splashbacks,' says designer David Hicks who reworked the apartment. One of the problems Hicks encountered was the service core areas in the apartment. 'Some of the core service areas couldn't be changed. I had to work around them,' says Hicks, who wanted to design something that was contemporary and comfortable. 'I also wanted to create a glamorous edge to the apartment,' he adds. The clients, who had left a large house in the suburbs, did not want to feel as though they were living in an apartment.

Therefore, to open up the space as much as possible, Hicks removed a high bench and storage cupboard from between the kitchen and living area. One wall of kitchen cupboards was also removed and replaced with a full-length mirror. Another wall was replaced with a bank of lacquered cupboards, concealing the pantry, fridge and cooking facilities. 'The mirror extends the feeling of space. At night, it reflects the view of the city,' he says. Even the sink, embedded in the island bench, was designed to fade from view. Made of Corian, like the benchtop, it was moulded to the unit.

As the one living area includes the kitchen, dining area and lounge, Hicks was mindful of the need for separation of function. Instead of a series of screens or divisions, the ceiling was redesigned with three distinct heights. Like the curved walls, which are angled to catch the view, the stepped ceiling gradually increases to 3 metres in the lounge area. 'It's a subtle way of defining the space,' he says.

The interior now compliments the building itself, elegant, striking and with that slight edge.

David Hicks Pty Ltd Design   Photography by Trevor Mein

47

An Artist's Retreat

This artist's studio is a freestanding building. Located in the backyard of a period-style home, the intention was to allow the owner, an artist, to have a complete retreat from the usual activities in her household.

In the backyard there was a dairy, originally used for the storage of milk. The redbrick dairy, built at the turn of the last century, was dark and inappropriate for an artist's studio. But it had a few substantial walls that could be incorporated into something new. Architect Michael Rahill's brief from the artist was to create a light-filled studio, a kitchen and a bathroom, together with a separate sleeping area. With a footprint of less than 50 square metres to work with, the spaces had to be designed with the greatest efficiency.

Rahill retained the height and shape of the skillion roof and simply replaced the weathered tin roof. He also inserted a new skylight, illuminating the interior. The architect looked at neighbouring homes in the area and was influenced by their corrugated additions. Instead of using some of the old bricks and rendering the surfaces, Rahill allowed the old bricks to be expressed clearly against the new corrugated steel.

Inside the building, the open-plan ground-floor space is defined by changes in ceiling heights. In the area used for painting, the ceiling height is approximately 3 metres. But in the kitchen and living area, the ceiling heights were reduced to just over 2 metres. 'I wanted to give the space a sense of composure and definition. It's only a small area and I didn't want it to feel as though there was only one space,' says Rahill, who tucked the loft-style bedroom into the existing roofline.

The result is a self-sufficient space, one that can be used independently from the house should guests stay over. Rahill included in the design a simple kitchen in black-and-white laminate. Two laminate 'boxes' attached to a wall and the main bench are simply elevated by two stainless-steel frames. 'There's a two-burner stove. My client makes her own canvases, so it's usually the smell of glue coming from the stove.'

Michael Rahill Architect   Photography by Martin Saunders and by Tom Campbell

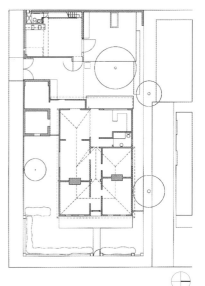

Look, No Walls!

This 1920s apartment is one of a group of four. Originally similar in layout to a long narrow terrace, consecutive rooms came off a passageway. 'Our clients wanted to move into the apartment and live in it for a while before renovating,' says Barry Ludlow of Neometro Architects. However, shortly after moving in, the clients realised a significant renovation was required. While the apartment overlooks a local park, only the living room had a leafy outlook. The rest of the rooms, including the kitchen, looked onto blank walls or neighbouring flats.

The architects removed as many internal walls as possible. The kitchen, which had been wedged in between the living and dining area, was combined into the one space. The ceiling height from the kitchen through to the bathroom was also raised, 'rolling up' to a generous 5 metres. A curved bulkhead, complete with an overhead skylight, increases the sense of volume in the apartment. 'We found the extra space in the roof,' says Ludlow.

As the apartment varies in width between 4 and 6 metres, the architects were keen to remove as much of the passage wall as possible. Even the doors to some of the rooms were removed to increase the individual spaces. 'We wanted to create a sense of flow through the apartment,' says Ludlow. The living/kitchen/dining area now extends across 14 metres and the view of the gardens can be more fully appreciated.

Dark timber stained panelling was incorporated into the new interior. 'There's a feel of the English gentlemen's club,' says Ludlow, who also removed some of the heavier period features in the apartment. The heavy and ornate timber over-mantle in the living area, for example, was substituted for a more contemporary fireplace. 'We wanted something lighter and simpler that nevertheless suggested the past,' he adds.

Neometro Architects   Photography by James Grant

common corridor

entry

living

kitchen

dining

roof light

w.i.r

bedroom 1

ensuite

powder

rear entry

existing walkway and stair

laundry

study

bedroom 2

terrace

fireplace

0   2m

External Rooms

A vacant site, measuring 8 by 20 metres, would not normally create great expectations. Nevertheless, the owner of this inner-city block expected considerably more than simply a small infill house. 'I wanted a house with architectural integrity. There wasn't a particular style on my mind, but I wanted something with a strong connection to the outdoors,' says the owner.

The house, made of concrete blocks, is not large. However, the architects have maximised the feeling of space by including cathedral ceilings in the living area. These ceilings bring natural light into the interior and eliminate the sight of neighbouring homes. There is no back garden and unlike most suburban homes, no plants at all. However, when the doors are left open, the external spaces do take on the feel of additional rooms.

Thinking of the home as an investment, the owner originally contemplated three bedrooms in the design. However, living on his own, it was suggested by Kennedy Nolan Architects, who designed the house, that he think of three additional 'spaces' rather than bedrooms instead. Like the main bedroom and large bathroom upstairs, which are spread over the second level, the two additional rooms downstairs are loosely defined, without doors. One space is currently used as a study and the other to listen to music.

The boundary between the kitchen and living area is also loosely defined. The kitchen features one continuous Oregon bench and a mirrored wall. The kitchen/dining room table was designed as the eating area. In warmer months, an outdoor barbeque in the central courtyard allows for alfresco dining.

An important part of the designer's brief was to explore the outdoors as a series of external rooms rather than as a garden. The garage, screened by timber battens to the street, doesn't have any of the usual features such as a workbench. 'It's a passive outdoor space. Any oil marks on the scoria can be raked over,' says architect Rachel Nolan. Even the wide passage, separating the main living area from the other 'spaces', has an outdoor feel, with a terrazzo floor, concrete wall and large timber sliding door to the central courtyard.

This house first appeared in Domain, *The Age* newspaper, 5 June 2002.

Kennedy Nolan Architects   Photography by Derek Swalwell

A Sense of Space

This single-fronted Victorian terrace had restricted views. On one side of the house was a two-storey brick wall and in the rear garden there were a series of outbuildings. In this renovation, the two front rooms were retained and the remainder of the house was completely redesigned. 'My client wanted a home office. He not only required a study, but also a separate room to keep his files. He also wanted somewhere for guests to stay,' says architect Marcus O'Reilly.

Instead of designing a rectilinear extension that followed the lines of the narrow site, O'Reilly centred the redevelopment along a curvaceous glass wall. The wall wraps around the new living, dining and kitchen areas, and continues through to the bathroom, located behind the kitchen. 'The curve removes the sense of confinement. The line disappears from sight. It appears to continue well into the distance,' says O'Reilly.

The kitchen, which is open to the living area, also benefits from the double-storey void above. 'The void (which looks up to the bridge and mezzanine area) compensates for the limited floor area. You feel as though you are standing in a two-storey space,' says O'Reilly.

In the dining area, there is also the sense of looking beyond a fixed wall. O'Reilly blurred the boundaries between the dining area and the narrow side garden by inserting a series of thick sheets of laminated glass into the timber flooring. Beneath the glass is a fishpond, where the owner can enjoy the constant flash of goldfish passing under his feet. 'The light bounces off the water and plays with the interior walls and ceilings,' says O'Reilly. Light is also drawn in from the second floor. Internal openings in the walls of the study and mezzanine help to extend the space without compromising on privacy.

The materials used in this design also add to the lightness of the space. A perforated steel-mesh landing on the second level allows light to penetrate into the house. The open-tread staircase with stainless-steel balustrade helps create a sense of space. As O'Reilly says, 'It's about borrowing space and light where possible. It could be from a void or even from the pond.'

Marcus O'Reilly Architect   Photography by Marcus O'Reilly

Extending the Angles

This project was a collaboration between architect James Brearley and artist Stephen Bram. Brearley saw some models Bram was working on and was keen to investigate some of these ideas in the built form. 'His models are about perspective and expanding the vantage point,' says Brearley.

For this townhouse, abutting a lane and behind a strip shopping centre, expanding the only vantage point seemed appropriate. Hemmed in from all sides, the site is only 7 metres wide by 15 metres in depth. Almost enclosed, the two-storey shell, which was part of a factory, only had two windows.

Instead of constructing walls to divide up the spaces, Brearley and Bram used perspective views to create the illusion of longer and shorter distances. The result was that a modest warehouse shell became a highly complex set of perceptions. 'We created a void over the two levels and inserted glass walls,' says Brearely. But the glass and steel window-walls were designed at an angle to the building. The remainder of the external space was then used as a courtyard. 'The angled walls bring in greater light and ventilation,' he adds.

On the ground floor are an entrance, two bedrooms, a bathroom and a mezzanine (tucked in between the two levels). On the first level is the kitchen and living area, separated by an oversized angular column. Like the angled walls, the ceiling heights have been manipulated to create a sense of space. The ceiling height in the entrance is only 2.4 metres. The designers chose to compress this area (using a dark coloured carpet, for example), as a contrast to the lighter more open spaces.

While the interior activates the senses, there is an overriding feeling of order. Although it's a highly complex environment, it is remarkably calm. The mind seems to sense the order without being able to immediately rationalise it. And while the views to the external environment remain restricted, the interior delights are stimulating.

**Brearley Architects and Urban Designers
with Stephen Bram, Artist**

Photography by Michael Goldsmith

A Tree House

Perched above two concrete water tanks, this small structure was designed as a retreat for the client. While the existing ranch-style homestead is relatively spacious, the owner wanted to build a completely separate area as a study and for when guests stay over. The architects Baenziger Coles wanted to complement the existing attributes of an elongated, ranch-style homestead.

The new house, referred to as the 'tree house', straddles two unsightly concrete water tanks. 'The tanks were just outside the back door. They look unsightly but they're still needed on the property,' says interior designer Bryn Holton of Baenziger Coles Architects. Rather than demolish or relocate the tanks, the architects used pine poles to elevate the new retreat to take advantage of the surrounding views of the forest. As the new structure skims over the tanks, access to water is still possible.

The new retreat is made of plywood and has a large eave to protect the interior from harsh light. 'It's like a cap on top of the ridgeline. It's similar in appearance to the existing house,' says Holton. Inside the retreat, which is linked to the main house by a veranda and staircase, is one space. Approximately 50 square metres in size, the space was designed with flexibility in mind. At one end is a table and chair. At the other end of the space is a more informal seating arrangement with a lounge and a couple of chairs. But if guests stay over, there's a mattress in the cupboard and the use of a small kitchenette.

While the tree house is located just outside the backdoor of the main house, it feels completely detached. With its small Juliet-style balcony, the views extend towards the rolling hills in the distance. Blade walls, attached to the exterior of the tree house, also screen views of the main house.

Baenziger Coles Architects   Photography by Rob Skovell

One Large Space

This studio-style warehouse apartment was originally part of a biscuit factory that was built in the 1860s. Recently, the factory was converted into 31 apartments, with two new levels added to the roof. While some of the spaces were fitted out and sold, others, such as this space were simply bought as a shell.

'It was basically only four walls, a sewerage point in one corner and some rough wiring,' says Shania Shegedyn, who bought the space to use as a home and photographic studio with her partner Tom McCallum. Both photographers, their requirement was for a light-filled space. They also both photograph architecture so they knew exactly what they wanted to achieve in this space.

Approximately 80 square metres in size, the space was left as open as possible. A change in floor levels is one of the few divisions made in the apartment. The passage to the main kitchen and living space is elevated, together with the bathroom and bedroom. 'We had to replace the old timber floors. The new acoustic sub-floor also conceals the plumbing,' says McCallum. Fortunately, many of the original features could be saved, such as the original timber joists supporting the floor above. Even the original brick walls were left partially exposed. 'We wanted to create a new layer to the space. But we also wanted to retain the history of the building,' says Shegedyn.

A kitchen was designed at one end of the space. The kitchen cupboards are made of a 'vinyl wrap' (similar to a satin-like laminate) and the bench is finished in concrete. 'We were thinking about a central bench but we appreciate the extra space and there's sufficient space for the two of us,' says Shegedyn.

The bedroom, defined only by a change in floor level, was also left open to the main living area. While there is the option of enclosing the space at a later date, the couple prefer the extra light entering the living area from the large bedroom window. And although the main bathroom is enclosed, the door is made of seraphic glass. Seraphic glass was also used to enclose the toilet within the bathroom. 'The space is entirely sealed but natural light can still penetrate,' says Shegedyn.

While the space is small, the couple were keen to make a few larger gestures. The width of the corridor, for example, is 1.5 metres wide and the doors (where provided) are floor to ceiling. Skirting boards were eliminated to maximise the dimensions of the space. 'We tried to keep the lines as clean as possible,' says McCallum, who included a large storage room immediately past the front door. 'Our photographic gear remains out of sight when we're not working.'

Shania Shegedyn Photographers

Photography by Shania Shegedyn and by Tom McCallum

A Small Space – A Large Project

This Victorian terrace was completely dilapidated before the architects moved in to redesign the space. 'The owners kept putting the renovation off. They were keen to do the entire renovation at the one time rather than as a series of incremental improvements over time,' says architect David Melocco of Melocco & Moore Architects.

Only 4 metres in width and with exceptionally poor light, the owners and architects agreed that an entirely new house was the best option. But with heritage restrictions in this inner-city area, it was prudent to retain the home's original façade, a few internal walls and a rear two-storey wall. Most of the internal walls were removed and the floor levels were adjusted, including the attic, to create more comfortable spaces.

One of the main problems was the orientation of the house, with the majority of light coming from the street, rather than from the backyard. To compensate for this orientation, the architects designed a series of 'finger pavilions', complete with concealed overhead skylights, along the boundary walls. The skylights appear in the new front living, dining and kitchen area. They also appear in the bedroom and bathroom on the first level.

For the small study, on the top level, the architects created a light-filled nook in an existing dormer-style window. 'We wanted to maximise the study space, rather than just provide a place to stand when you reached the top of the stairs,' says Melocco, who designed a built-in lounge and storage cupboard underneath.

The height and scale of the joinery in the house was designed to provide a continuous line from the front door to the back patio. The joinery creates the same rhythmic quality to the space, with the proportions of the cabinet in the living area echoing the scale of the cabinets in the kitchen. The kitchen bench gives the impression of being elevated above the timber floors, concealed lighting under the bench creating a floating effect.

The house, designed for a couple, includes a new outdoor courtyard. While this space isn't large, the architects used horizontal timber slats along one wall as a backdrop. The cascading concrete stairs, featuring a narrow slot-like two-tiered pond, extends the view to the rear of the site. A refined model for terrace living, there's a quality of space that belies the restraints of the site.

Melocco & Moore Architects Pty Ltd   Photography by Paul Gosney

A Small Gem

This house, located on a small block measuring 3.8 metres by 25 metres, is sensitively placed within a row of Victorian-style terraces. The house, designed by O'Connor and Houle Architects, comprises three storeys and is located within a tightly regulated heritage streetscape. Its exterior form or general massing borrows from its Victorian neighbours. It is built to the street without any setback and its height matches that of its neighbours, albeit being three storeys rather than a more typical two-storey terrace.

Because of the narrow dimensions of the site, the architects relied on the vertical dimensions of the house to create a number of experiences. For example, the library at the front of the house is 5 metres in height, allowing bookshelves abutting the front translucent window onto the street, to span two levels of the house. At night the library is backlit and offers shadows of books to the street. A small study, located on the mezzanine level overlooks the library, sheltering a more intimate sitting area below.

The bedroom ceilings are a standard 2.4 metres and create a sense of intimacy. The kitchen-living area is 3.3 metres in height, providing plenty of breathing space. Large floor-to-ceiling doors open out to the garden and offer a continuum between indoors and outdoors.

Unlike many terrace-style houses that have a dark central core, this new house was designed around a central light well, which brings light into the middle section of the house. Two compact bathrooms are located adjacent to the stair and gain their light through translucent glass interior windows.

This small house almost disappears from the streetscape. There are no ornate trimmings on the façade and many passers-by would simply not turn their heads. But once inside the front door, the spaces immediately impress and the surprises continue at every turn.

This house first appeared in Australian *Vogue Living* magazine, April/May issue, 2000.

O'Connor + Houle Architecture

Photography by Peter Clarke

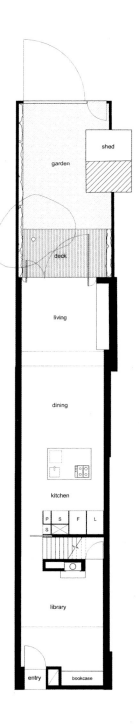

garden

shed

deck

living

dining

kitchen

P S F L
S

library

entry   bookcase

73

roof

deck

bedroom 3

robe

bath 2

storage

study

desk

void

deck

bedroom 2

bath 1

L

robe

bedroom 1

seat

Going Vertical

The owners of this inner-city terrace couldn't decide whether or not to stay or move to a larger house. On a corner site, the three-level house is wedged into 50 square metres of space. 'It tapers off to less than a couple of metres at the rear,' says architect Stephen Varady, who redesigned the house.

On the ground level are two bedrooms, a bathroom and laundry. On the second level is the living and kitchen area and the third is now an additional bedroom, ensuite and deck. There's also a fourth level, the roof deck that spans across the entire building. Originally, the third level was a study. But the owners were keen to use the top level as their main bedroom, to both increase the number of bedrooms and to maximise enjoyment of the surrounding views from the roof deck.

As space was limited and there was not sufficient room for a usual bedroom (encased with walls), Varady designed a bedroom on a platform. Half of the bed is supported on a plinth that contains storage and the other half is cantilevered over the stairwell. 'I did suggest creating a bed-end in thickened glass. But the owners preferred to keep the bed open to the stairwell,' says Varady. While the bedroom is just over a metre from the ceiling, there's a deep skylight overhead to extend the space and bring in additional light.

Directly behind the elevated bed is possibly one of the smallest bathrooms ever designed. Encased in colour-back glass (floors and walls), the glass shower door must be kept open in order to use the toilet. As Varady says, 'My clients loved the position of the house but they needed an extra bedroom. It really was a matter of trying to insert an additional bedroom and still make the house feel large enough for a small family.'

Stephen Varady Architecture   Photography by Stephen Varady

A Number of Options

This inner-city site in a semi-industrial area was previously a factory. When the factory was pulled down, eight townhouses were constructed. Rather than create one configuration and one townhouse, the architects were keen to offer a range of accommodation. 'They vary in size from 120 to 240 square metres,' says architect David Neil. 'We wanted to create generous spaces and include quality fittings,' he adds.

This townhouse, which is one of the smallest in the group, is designed over four levels. On the ground level is a home office for the owner, an interior designer. On the first floor is the kitchen, living and small balcony. The two bedrooms are on the second level and on the top level, is a generous roof garden, with spectacular views of the city.

The office on the ground floor provides a self-contained area for clients. There's direct access from the street and it is completely separated from the living areas above. The kitchen, directly above, was conceived as one open space. There isn't even the usual island bench. It is tucked into the end of the space. 'We wanted to make sure there was room for a dining table and an informal area for sitting,' says Neil, who also included a small balcony with sufficient room to place a few chairs.

In the living area, Neil designed a ledge/buffet to store tableware and for the display of flowers. 'We wanted to reduce the amount of furniture that was needed. It gives this area a more spacious feel.'

There are two bedrooms on the second floor, the main bedroom, and a smaller second bedroom. Only one of the bedrooms is currently used, the second is a study. To maximise space in the study, a large sliding door was designed. 'When it's left open, it combines with the space in the hallway,' says Neil. The sense of space is also increased with the open timber staircase that links each level. The steel-grid mesh landings on each level bring in natural light throughout the townhouse.

David Neil Architects   Photography by Shannon McGrath

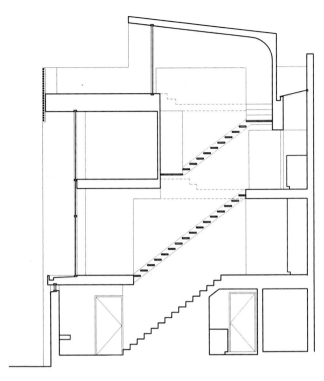

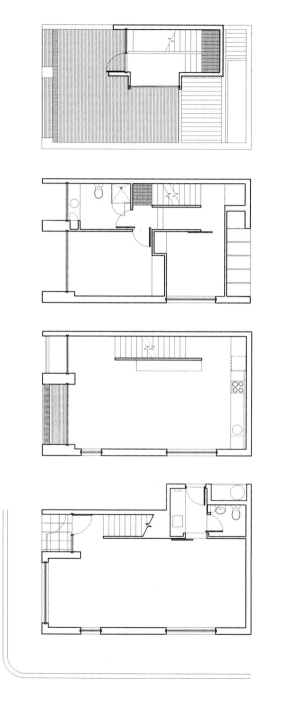

Extending a Cottage

This cottage, approximately 5 metres wide, originally consisted of three rooms off a central passage. A kitchen, bathroom and enclosed veranda had been tacked onto the back of the house. Built in 1905, the house required considerable updating which included some new windows, rewiring and a new roof.

Utz-Sanby Architects removed the later additions and created an entirely new living wing. Set on a polished concrete floor, the extension accommodates a dining, kitchen and living area, with large folding doors to a rear terrace. New bathroom, laundry and deck areas were inserted between the original part of the house and the new living areas.

Clad in galvanised mini-orb, there is a strong delineation between the old and the new styles. The roof of the bathroom and laundry area (referred to as the link) was designed flat, in contrast to the pitched corrugated roofs of the original house and the new pavilion. The end gables of the new pavilion were also deliberately glazed. From the living room, the view of the pitched roof can be appreciated. 'The gable also allows the light to penetrate into the living areas,' says architect Kristen Utz.

The open-plan living space has been divided into a dining area, kitchen and living area. The timber columns framing the space outline each area, as do the kitchen walls (1.2 metres in height) that conceal the benchtops. 'When you are sitting in the living area, you're not reminded of the kitchen,' says Utz, who also designed the laundry to be screened from view when not in use. The laundry, concealed behind sliding doors, features a 3-metre-long bench and an internal clothesline. When extra space is required, a small portion of the living area can be used as a working space.

The new pavilion also features 4-metre-high ceilings (to the apex). While the new wing is contemporary, it makes clear references to the original cottage, both in size and proportion.

Utz-Sanby Architects   Photography by Ray Clarke

A Sense of Privacy

On a site measuring only 164 square metres, the architects managed to design five apartments, three two-bedroom apartments (98 square metres) and two one-bedroom (44 square metres). Yet even with this density, there is a sense of privacy.

Designed by Architects Johannsen + Associates, the development was originally intended as a mixture of commercial and residential spaces. But with strong demand for inner-city apartments, the land was rezoned for residential purposes.

The site was extremely small and the area dense, so even building the townhouses was problematic. As there was no room for storage of building materials on site, the building was made of entirely precast panels. All the walls, for example, were erected in three days.

The apartments directly abut the footpath so the architects were keen to 'layer' the internal spaces and blur the division between the indoor and outdoor areas of the apartments. 'We created a number of double-height courtyards on the site, with balconies overhanging these areas. Once you have passed the front gate, you're not aware of the proximity to the street,' says architect Gaby Gering.

One of the two-bedroom apartments features a garage or studio space on the ground level (depending on whether the car is parked or left on the street). There is a bedroom, laundry and bathroom on the first floor, together with a small balcony that juts into the double-voided courtyard. On the second floor is the kitchen, dining and living area, also with a balcony, considerably larger in size. And the third level is given over to the main bedroom and ensuite. There is also a balcony outside the main bedroom. 'The balconies increase the sense of space, both in a visual as well as functional sense,' says Gering.

One of the other ways of creating a sense of space and increasing the ventilation was by designing an open timber-tread staircase that links the levels. Instead of enclosing this core with a balustrade, the architects designed an open staircase with steel rods. Light can enter the lower levels and the open treads improve the ventilation in the townhouse.

Architects Johannsen + Associates Pty Ltd

Photography by Anthony Fretwell

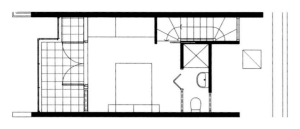

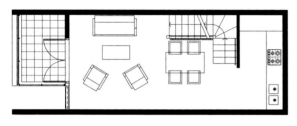

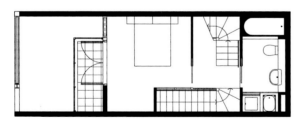

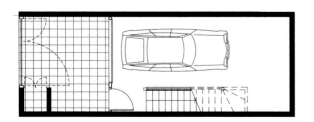

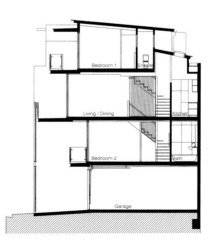

Four Metres Wide

This narrow terrace originally consisted of two rooms at the front of the house, a dining area and a kitchen. In the 1960s, when the house was renovated, the owners added a brick bathroom and laundry. While the new addition was more convenient, it eliminated any light entering the home. 'There was no connection to the backyard. And it's where most of the light comes from,' says architect David Stevenson, of the practice Lacoste + Stevenson.

The 1960s additions were completely removed and bathroom/laundry facilities were incorporated into the new design. The design also included removing one of the small bedrooms. A new and larger bedroom with a study area was provided on the first floor along with a roof terrace. The second bedroom on the ground level was used to increase the size of the living areas. The remainder of the space was left open. 'You can see the back terrace as soon as you open the front door,' says Stevenson. 'We deliberately designed the staircase with open treads to allow for a continuous view,' he adds. And to further increase the connection to the rear yard, full-length bi-fold doors were installed, capable of being pulled right back during the warmer months.

To maximise space, the architects built the new kitchen to the boundaries of the site. A single bench with cupboards was designed on one side of the kitchen. On the other side is a bank of stained veneer cupboards that conceal the laundry, pantry and fridge. The architects used the back of these kitchen cupboards as storage areas for the bathroom behind. The bathroom features a full-length louvred glass window-wall to frame the shower.

The materials used in the renovation were selected for their light and transparent feeling. Polished concrete was used for the floors and colour-backed glass was used for the wet areas such as in the kitchen and bathroom. A light-coloured terrazzo was also used for the bench in the kitchen. 'These materials also reflect the light. We have even included glass on the reveals of the joinery,' says Stevenson.

Lacoste + Stevenson Architects   Photography by Marcus Clinton

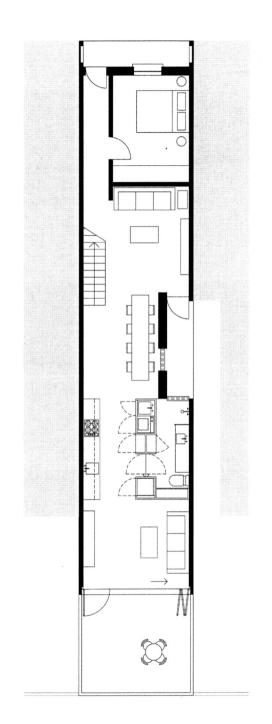

A Difficult Site

This triangular-shaped corner site is only 180 square metres in size. While the size of the site created considerable constraints, so did its geometry. 'How do you work with so many acute angles?' says architect George Yiontis, who with his partner Rosa Coy, also an architect, designed the house as their own home. 'Our approach was that there was no inside or outside. The perimeter wall would define the house,' says Yiontis.

A high brick wall was built for the perimeter, to create privacy from the busy corner site and to act as a sound barrier. 'The wall is prone to graffiti, but it can be easily removed from the bricks with a high-pressure hose,' says Yiontis. The wall also allows the external space to be incorporated into the open-plan living, kitchen and dining area. The parent's retreat (adjacent to the living areas) is strongly linked to the small courtyard too. A cantilevered concrete bench in the parent's retreat, which forms a plinth for the fireplace, doubles as seating for the outdoor space when the large glass windows are retracted.

The kitchen, dining and living area is open plan and behind the bank of cupboards that frame this space is the powder room and storage for the children's toys. Within this line of cupboards is a built-in daybed, eliminating the need for furniture in the living area. 'Maximising storage is essential in small spaces. There's a fine balance between making sure everything fits and making a space feel crowded with cupboards,' says Yiontis.

The staircase to the first floor is concealed behind a cupboard door. On the first floor is the main bedroom and two children's bedrooms. Instead of traditional doors, the architects used large sliding doors that can be drawn into the cavity walls. 'The passage space can be included in the bedroom space for extra room,' says Yiontis. And to create additional space in the bedrooms, the wardrobes face into the passageway, as does the laundry that is concealed behind a cupboard. 'The corridor is wider than normal (1.4 metres). When the laundry cupboards are open, this extra width creates additional work room. When the space isn't being used for ironing, it becomes additional space for the children to play,' he says.

And even when you think you have seen everything in the house, you stumble across a small study on the ground floor, accessed only through the parent's retreat. Nestled behind the high brick wall, its triangular shape echoes the shape of this small irregular block.

Coy & Yiontis Architects   Photography by Peter Clarke

96

A Stable

This warehouse was previously a stable. More recently, the property was used as a car repair workshop, with cars piled into the rear courtyard. As the total land area is only 86 square metres (including the courtyard), the architects were keen to include a third level into the renovation. 'We were surrounded by two-storey homes. But it wouldn't have been a proposition for my clients if we weren't able to obtain permission for a third level,' says architect Rob Brown of Dawson Brown Architecture.

The ground level, which included original timber doors, was redesigned with space for a car. Adjacent to this space and separated by a translucent glass wall, are the bathroom, dressing room and cellar. On the second floor is the open-plan living and dining area, together with the kitchen. One entire wall, lined with built-in bookshelves, defines the sitting area. On the third floor, added by the architects, is the main bedroom. 'The space was so tight. We had to place the bathroom and dressing area on the ground level,' says Brown. But while the owners do not have an ensuite, they do have access to a large roof terrace, immediately outside the main bedroom.

The architects were keen to retain as much of the original fabric of the building as possible. And where new materials were required, they were selected for their industrial aesthetic. A large steel and glass garage-style door, for example, links the bedroom to the terrace. Industrial steel treads were used for the staircase and recycled timber was used for the floors and the cupboards. The original timber stable doors were also retained in the renovation. But the doors were redesigned to form one sliding door and a front door was included within it.

While the footprint of the building couldn't be increased, the vertical space certainly could. And although the space is relatively small, it feels spacious. As Brown says, 'It was important to remove as many walls as possible and to maximise the light entering the space. The perforated treads (staircase) allow light to filter to the ground level.'

Dawson Brown Architecture   Photography by Richard Powers and by Rob Brown

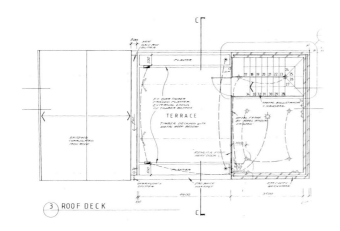

③ ROOF DECK

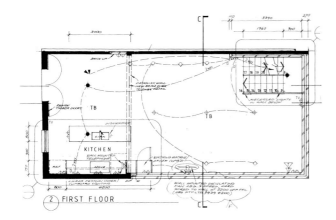

② FIRST FLOOR

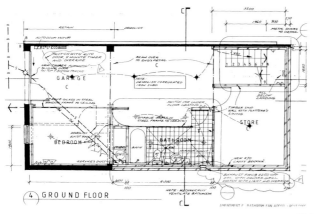

④ GROUND FLOOR

The Right Context

This new townhouse is surrounded by single-storey weatherboard terrace homes. In an inner-city beachside suburb, Holan Joubert Architects were interested in making a few coastal references. The materials selected have a coastal ambience. The first floor of the house is made of marine plywood. And some of the internal walls and the first floor are made of concrete block. 'The blocks are quite soft in appearance. They are also quite bleached,' says Holan. 'We're less than 2 kilometres from the beach. I thought it was an appropriate response.'

As the site is only 6.3 metres wide by 23 metres in depth, every aspect of the design was considered to the nth degree. At the front of the house there was just enough room for one car parking space, and the letterbox and paper drop had to be built into the front gate. But there was sufficient room in the front garden to design a couple of planter boxes and accommodate a small pond. 'It cools down the living area, particularly in the warmer months. It also has that restful quality,' says Holan.

Apart from a small timber-lined vestibule immediately past the front door, the kitchen, dining and living areas are completely open. Only the central atrium is enclosed. Lined with concrete blocks, the glass atrium acts as a light well. The concrete blocks absorb the heat and create a thermal mass during the winter months. In summer, a roof window can be opened up to release the heat. The atrium also doubles as a music room for Holan. Featuring laminated glass, this space has a special acoustic quality.

Behind the atrium are two bedrooms (or one bedroom and a study) that lead to a small rear courtyard garden. Upstairs, there is a main bedroom that cantilevers over the ground floor, as well as a bathroom, a study desk, and a small library, accessible by a nautical-style ladder.

While the house is compact, Holan was able to maximise the space by reducing corridors wherever possible. As Holan says, 'Very little has been left to waste. Even the spice shelves to the kitchen are created from a shallow recess in the block courtyard wall.'

Holan Joubert Architects   Photography by Peter Hyatt

Capitalising on the Position

This apartment occupies a privileged position overlooking Sydney's magical harbour. But apart from the view from the top floor of a six-storey building, it was disappointing. Built only two years ago, the interior already looked tired, although it had hardly been occupied.

One of the main problems was the height of the ceilings. The developer had located the main air-conditioning unit in the ceiling, which meant that the ceilings were as low as 2 metres in places. At only 80 square metres in size, the apartment also suffered from too much segmentation of the space. 'Our clients are a professional couple. They wanted a place that was open plan, but that could be compartmentalised should there be a need,' says architect Tony Chenchow of Chenchow Little Architects. 'One of the owners works occasionally at home. And friends and family may stay over,' says Chenchow.

One of the first things to be repositioned was the air-conditioning unit. It was removed from the ceiling space and relocated to the laundry core. While the laundry's ceiling remains at 2 metres, the rest of the ceiling could be significantly elevated to 2.5 metres. A double-height void over the main living area (5 metres) represented one of the few attractive elements that existed prior to renovation.

The wall enclosing the bathrooms was mirrored and the bathroom doors were designed flush with the wall. 'We wanted to create the illusion of space and this was where the space was most needed,' says Chenchow. The architects also removed the door from the second bedroom and created one large sliding door that can be pulled right back. 'It's a flexible space. It doesn't have to be closed off,' he adds.

Storage was another problem in this apartment. Keen to address this issue, the architects designed a wall starting from the kitchen and continuing through to the living space. Bookshelves are an integral part of this wall. Bottles and food items are displayed on kitchen shelves, while CDs, magazines and books appear on living-room shelves.

As Chenchow says, 'The design is about flexibility. Rooms can be closed up but it's a more exciting space when everything is left open.'

Chenchow Little Architects   Photography by Bart Maiorana

No Doors

This warehouse was built in the 1940s. The cream brick building has had a number of uses over the years. Its last reconfiguration was a nightclub in the 1980s. There was even carpet on all the walls to deaden the sound.

Surrounded by high-rise apartments and factories, the appeal of the warehouse was its size (270 square metres) and the light it received on the second floor of the building. 'Our clients wanted a warehouse-style of living. They didn't want a glorified apartment,' says architect Stephen Jolson, whose office was given the brief.

Separate toilets, one of the remaining legacies of the nightclub, were removed and the entire space was gutted. 'We didn't want to touch any of the existing walls, the floors or the ceiling (including the aluminium ducts),' says Jolson. 'The idea was like a semi-trailer that had come to be lodged in a warehouse,' says Jolson, referring to the pod-like rooms placed on an angle in the space.

Two zones were designed in the warehouse, one public and the other private. The public zone features the open-plan living area and the dining/kitchen area. The private zone features the two bedrooms, bathroom and laundry. 'Our clients stipulated they didn't want any doors,' says Jolson. However, there is one door in the corner of the kitchen area that leads to the laundry and bedroom areas. But this door is concealed in the kitchen, which features Statuaria marble benchtops and splashbacks. Like the secret door, the oven, dishwasher, fridge and pantry, are all concealed behind Imperite cupboards.

The architects incorporated an elevated timber platform as a base for the kitchen/dining area and the bedrooms. This floor, which has a stage-like appearance, also conceals the services such as plumbing and wiring.

For the two bedrooms (used by the owners as a bedroom and a study) curtains provide a substitute for doors and walls. The internal 'wall' of the main bedroom for example was wrapped with drapes. One side has full block-out and the other side is sheer. 'It's like a veil. It was about creating privacy, but also adding a softer and more tactile layer in the space.'

Stephen Jolson Architect   Photography by Tim Griffith

Reworking the Past

This double-fronted Victorian house was added to in the 1970s. With little consideration for the amount of light entering the home, the extension simply created a dark box. 'The extension was built boundary to boundary. The only natural light came from a small light court between the extension and the period home,' says architect Sally Draper of Swaney Draper Architects.

While the 1970s addition was no longer appropriate to the owner's needs, it did include a first-floor balcony and a floor-to-ceiling glass wall overlooking the rear garden. 'We decided to keep the 1970s shell for these reasons (council regulations would now restrict these features to ensure the neighbour's privacy). There were also budget considerations. It was more economical to work within the shell of the building,' adds Draper.

The 1970s shell was completely gutted and opened up to the single-storey part of the house. A large light court was cut through the two-storey addition, linking the old to the new work. A series of broad shallow stairs was also designed as a link. 'It was important to create circulation points in the house, which gave the sense of movement,' says Draper. The broad stairs are a contrast to the original staircase to the second floor, which is now concealed behind a blade wall. 'You can look back at the top of the staircase into the void. It gives you a new perspective of the space.'

What was once a series of dark rooms – the old kitchen, bathroom, separate living and dining room – has been opened entirely to the rear garden. The kitchen now occupies one side of the space, the living area the other. A generous skylight above the kitchen bench draws additional light into the space. The architects deliberately placed some elements off centre, such as the kitchen bench and fireplace in the living area. 'We were conscious of things appearing to flow in the space. Aligning everything up to be central would have created static in the space,' says Draper.

Just like the 1970s addition, (now rendered and finely detailed with steel), the original part of the house has also been opened up. One of the bedrooms has been converted into a dining room, the other into a bathroom and laundry. And while the footprint of the house hasn't changed, the feeling of space certainly has.

Swaney Draper Pty Ltd Architects   Photography by Shannon McGrath and by Peter Hyatt

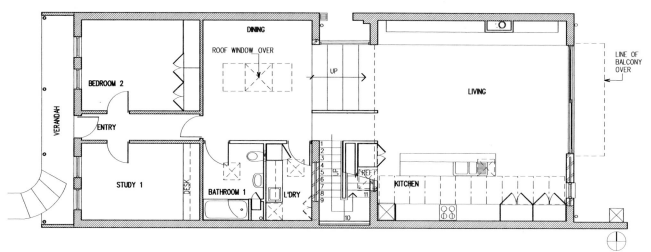

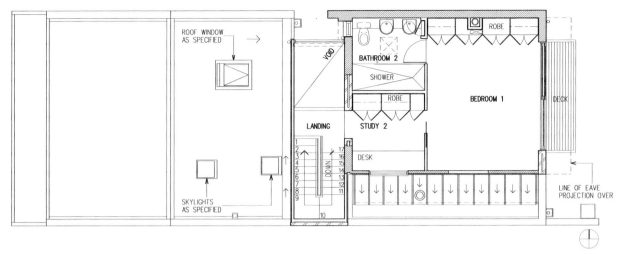

ROOF WINDOW
AS SPECIFIED →

VOID

BATHROOM 2

SHOWER

ROBE

LANDING

STUDY 2

DESK

SKYLIGHTS
AS SPECIFIED

DOWN

ROBE

BEDROOM 1

DECK

DESK

LINE OF EAVE
PROJECTION OVER

Robust

Located in a prime retail precinct, this site behind a corner store stood vacant for years. 'It's an area that has become increasing popular for young people,' says architect Michael Bialek of SJB Architects.

The heritage-listed store was restored and the vacant site was transformed into five apartments, spread over a three-level building. To provide a choice of accommodation, the architects designed one- and two-bedroom apartments, with the smallest being approximately 50 square metres.

The location of these apartments is relatively harsh. There's a railway cutting directly opposite and factories nearby. 'We wanted to design a robust building. Something that would stand up to the environment,' says Bialek. The building was constructed in precast concrete. There is a concrete floor in the lobby area and glass panels enclosing the communal stairwell. And to create a protective layer for the apartments, SJB Architects designed a series of monumental external timber battened screens across the building's façade. 'We built to the boundaries. We needed something that would screen the passing traffic, as well as the train,' says Bialek. The screens, framing the balconies, also protect the occupants from the sun. 'They filter the harsher light.'

Though the internal spaces are compact, they are well conceived. The kitchen and bathroom were deliberately designed in one core of the apartment to maximise the space. And while the kitchen is open to the main living spaces, it is well defined by a floating bench that cantilevers out from the kitchen.

The views of the city in the distance are panoramic. As Bialek says, 'We tried to maximise the views from all the apartments. It's only when you enter these spaces that you can truly appreciate this location.'

SJB Architects   Photography by Tony Miller

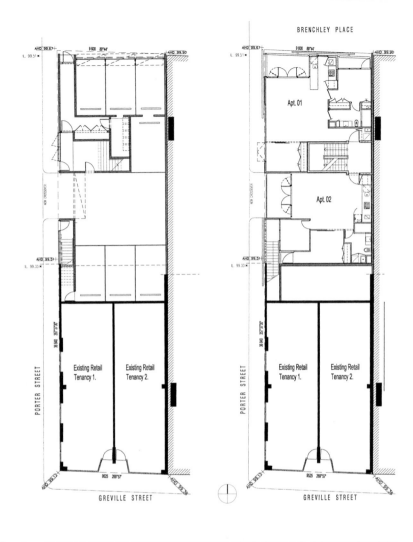

BRENCHLEY PLACE

Apt. 01

Apt. 02

Existing Retail
Tenancy 1.

Existing Retail
Tenancy 2.

PORTER STREET

GREVILLE STREET

Existing Retail
Tenancy 1.

Existing Retail
Tenancy 2.

PORTER STREET

GREVILLE STREET

BRENCHLEY PL

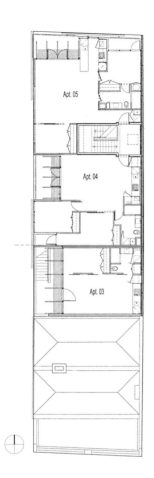

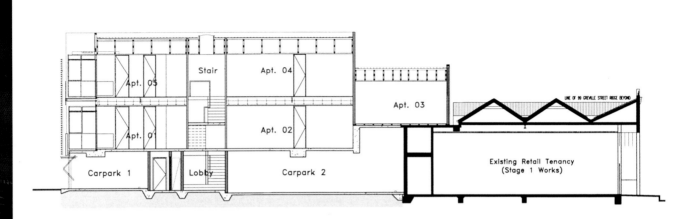

Apt. 05   Stair   Apt. 04

Apt. 03

LINE OF 99 GREVILLE STREET RIDGE BEYOND

Apt. 01   Apt. 02

Carpark 1   Lobby   Carpark 2

Existing Retail Tenancy
(Stage 1 Works)

A Federation Terrace

This terrace, built at the turn of the last century, was claustrophobic and had poor connections to outdoor spaces. While new spaces have been added to the house, old ones have also been completely opened up to create a lighter and more transparent house. What was once a small cottage is now a family home with three bedrooms.

As the site is a typically small inner-city site, 5 metres wide by 25 metres in depth, it was not possible to enlarge the footprint of the house. A second storey was the best solution so a new second-storey bedroom and bathroom were added to the terrace.

While there is continuity between the old and new spaces, the new work can be read easily. 'The historical layering of nearly 100 years of additions and alterations are an important part of the historical makeup of the building,' says architect Annabel Lahz of Lahz Nimmo Architects. The original two front rooms of the house were kept intact. But the new work is unashamedly modern. 'The design is essentially two plywood boxes, detailed to have a furniture-like quality,' says Lahz. One of the boxes contains the bedroom and sits astride the existing masonry house. The other contains the bathroom, which is interlocked into the larger of the two boxes. 'By lifting the bathroom off the ground plain, you are able to look through the entire space on the ground floor,' she adds.

It was also important to increase the amount of natural light in the house. Highlights to the second level bathroom throw a gentle light across the hoop pine ceiling. And timber battens, under a polycarbonate roof to the bathroom, cast sharp lines of shadow across the tiled walls and floor. 'It feels like you're bathing in an outdoor pergola,' says Lahz.

The internal renovations involved the removal of cross walls to make one large room that contains the living, dining and kitchen areas. The removal of walls also allowed a visual connection to the courtyard from the front door.

Lahz Nimmo Architects Pty Ltd   Photography by Brett Boardman

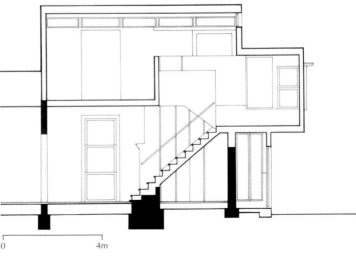

0   4m

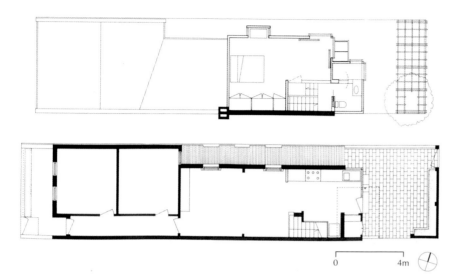

Upside Down House

This 1920s row house in the inner city has been completely reworked by architect David Luck. The two-storey home originally had an open living area on the ground floor and two bedrooms on the first floor. But with more light on the first floor and city views, it was decided to completely reverse the layout. 'I refer to it as the upside down house,' says Luck, who transformed the dark period house into a light and contemporary space.

In contrast to the current trend of removing walls, Luck enclosed the spaces on the ground floor to form two bedrooms. Solid MDF sliding doors between the bedrooms and passage reverted the house back to its terrace-like form, with a corridor down one side of the house and rooms to one side.

However, on the first floor, which was previously used as two bedrooms, walls were removed. Even the floor-to-ceiling walls encasing the staircase on the second level were removed. Luck designed two units on either side of the staircase. One faces the living area and functions as a writing desk. The other unit, facing the dining area, was designed to store crockery.

Luck also built upon the original footprint of the house, by rebuilding a rear carport and designing a new kitchen above it. One of the main concerns with the new addition was privacy. To comply with council regulations, Luck framed the new roof deck with Colorbond cladding. A canopy, made of the same material, was designed to screen the sunlight and add privacy. 'It floats above the deck. It creates a sense of lightness,' says Luck, who used the same russet colour for the canopy as for a bank of cupboards in the kitchen. 'The colour connects the elements. It creates a tighter composition,' says Luck.

While the house has only been increased slightly in size, the space feels significantly larger. As Luck says, 'It's important to get as much light into a house as possible. If there is insufficient room for windows, you need to rely on reflective light and reflective surfaces.'

David Luck Architecture   Photography by Graeme Schrapnel and by David Luck

Small Changes

This inner-city villa had been extensively renovated in the eighties. While some of the finishes and colour schemes had dated, other features were still functional 20 years later. 'The extension was in the postmodern style. It's not what architects design now, but the extension was well built and orientated to the light,' says architect Richard Swansson, who modernised the 1980s finishes and changed the powder-blue walls. 'We reworked some of the joinery and updated the appliances. But we didn't see the point of starting all over,' he says.

Fortunately, the previous owners also had the foresight to include two small courtyards on either side of the passage, between the original house and the new wing. But while light filtered into the core of the house, a solid wall separated the main bathroom from the dressing area and ensuite bathroom, leaving both spaces formidable places. Swansson removed the wall in the main bathroom and inserted a new steel and glass wall. The top part of the new wall is clear glass, the lower portion frosted. 'You can see the silhouette when someone is getting dressed,' says Swansson, whose clients are a professional couple. The windows in the bathroom were also extended to the floor to create additional light.

As the project was for a couple who have family staying over occasionally, the architect was able to include a glass-walled shower in the courtyard leading from the dressing area. 'The feeling is like showering in the garden,' says Swansson. In the other courtyard, on the opposite side of the passage, Swansson inserted a small reflective pool. Adjacent to the living area, the dappled light reflected from the water plays upon the interior walls. As Swansson says, 'With small spaces, you need to simplify things. You need to create a sense of clarity.'

Richard Swansson Architect   Photography by Derek Swalwell

Removing the Divisions

This semi-detached house, one of a row of six, required a new wing. The only two rooms left in their original form were the two bedrooms at the front of the house. While the third room, the dining room, was in reasonably good order, the owners didn't require a separate room for formal entertaining. As a result, the architects Black Kosloff Knott (BKK) removed the walls in the dining room and incorporated this space into a new study, kitchen and living area. 'We've only increased the footprint of the building by 2 metres,' says architect Simon Knott.

As the width of the house is only 5 metres, the architects used joinery in the new section to suggest rooms. Where the dining room used to be, there is now a study, which takes the form of a separate module (there is a 600-millimetre gap between the study wall and the ceiling). The architects also created an unusual glass door to further screen the study. The door is digitally screen-printed with the image of a curtain. The study wall facing the kitchen and living area was designed as a bank of cupboards. The pantry, fridge and valuable storage area are screened from view.

The main bench in the space functions as both a kitchen bench and a dining room table. With a change in level of one step between the two ends, the table cantilevers over the living room floor. And beyond that point, the other bench emerges in the courtyard, taking the form of an outdoor barbecue.

Built-in shelving on the other side of the living space was designed as a series of boxes, with every 'container' marginally larger in size at it approaches the rear of the space. As architect Tim Black says, 'It creates a perspective and a certain rhythm. The uses appear to evolve as you move through the space. The idea was to suggest a series of rooms.'

Black Kosloff Knott Pty Ltd   Photography by Craig Wood

Enhancing the Views

This ninth-floor apartment, overlooking Sydney harbour, could have been anywhere. Spectacular views were largely concealed by a long central passage running through it. The views from the balconies were also disjointed. 'It was dark and the rooms were disconnected. The balconies were too narrow to be used (1 metre in width),' says architect Andrew Stanic of Stanic Harding Architects.

As the owners only required two bedrooms, the third bedroom was converted into a study. With its new angular wall, the study follows the line of the entry alcove. 'We wanted to include strong diagonal lines and make some important connections to the edge of the apartment, where the views and the light are most intense,' says Stanic.

The new kitchen was also opened out to the main living space, delineated only by a small change in floor level. 'The platform is only 110 millimetres high. But it creates an important division,' says Stanic, who also elevated the main bedroom, dressing area and ensuite. 'The platform allows you to conceal services such as plumbing,' he adds.

One of the most significant aspects of the renovation was to enclose the balcony adjacent to the living area. Located on the ninth floor, this outdoor area was more of a wind tunnel than a place to enjoy the harbour views. However, mindful of the need for ventilation and wanting to make a strong connection to the exterior space, the architects installed a bank of glass louvred windows. And the toughened glass balustrade designed on the inside of the louvres acts as a safety measure. With 25 metres of additional space, the dining/living area is now one spacious area.

The main bedroom was also reconfigured, with the bedroom, rather than the bathroom affording the best views. Stanic Harding relocated the doorway to the bedroom further from the main living area. 'It's now like a private suite,' says Stanic, who also included a mirrored wall outside the main bedroom. 'At night the view is reflected back into the apartment. It's quite magical.'

Stanic Harding Pty Ltd   Photography by Paul Gosney

A Backyard

This townhouse was built behind a worker's cottage. The architects renovated the cottage, subdivided the land, and built a new three-storey townhouse in the backyard. As the cottage backed onto a small street, the new townhouse was able to have its own street frontage.

Located in a semi-industrial inner-city area, the 'backyard' site only measures 7 by 15 metres. 'The dimensions were extremely tight. The only way to make it work was to design three levels,' says architect Jane McDougall of Alsocan Architects. The rendered masonry townhouse occupies almost the entire site. A couple of metres in one corner of the site were allocated for a small courtyard garden. Another portion of land in the centre of the site acts as a light well for the townhouse.

There are two bedrooms on the ground level, together with a bathroom. There is also sufficient space to provide car parking for two cars in tandem. On the first floor are the open-plan kitchen, living and dining area, and on the third floor is the main bedroom. To allow the client to appreciate the city skyline, Alsocan included two terraces, one adjacent to the living area, and a smaller terrace on the third level. 'We tried to make the spaces as open plan as possible. The main focus is through the windows at either end of the spaces,' says McDougall.

While the kitchen is open plan, it is loosely defined by a central bench and hanging shelves, suspended from stainless-steel rods. The veneered kitchen cupboards also feature glass interlay, adding a transparency to the kitchen. To link the second level to the main bedroom above, the architects incorporated a stainless-steel spiral staircase. 'The floor area is reasonably tight. A staircase any larger would have appeared out of scale with these spaces,' says McDougall.

Even the main bedroom and bathroom have been reduced to one open space. The only division is the change in flooring, timber for the bedroom and tiles for the bathroom. A toughened glass shower screen over the bath is one of the few obvious divisions.

Alsocan Architects   Photography by David Beynon

The Same Footprint

Originally, there was a small fibro cottage on this site. Built in the 1920s, restoring the house was simply not an option but the owners were keen to retain its scale. 'Their brief was "a house on holidays,"' says architect Mark Jones. 'We retained the original footprint, but everything from the ground floor up was entirely rebuilt,' he adds.

The architects used fibro sheets to create the new structure. These sheets have been clad with horizontal timber battens and, like the house, feature a corrugated metal roof.

While the house is relatively compact (approximately 120 square metres in total), it was designed to maximise the space. The living spaces appear larger as the architects have focused on the bushland views. They have also maximised the floor space by designing two attic-style bedrooms under the new corrugated steel roof, one pitched, the other curved.

The house includes an open-plan kitchen, living and dining area on the ground floor, together with a bathroom. On the first floor there are two bedrooms, one large mezzanine-style bedroom, the other smaller and enclosed. The larger of the upstairs bedrooms overlooks the living areas below. But while the smaller of the upstairs bedrooms is enclosed, the focus is on the curved corrugated metal. 'It creates a sense of the unexpected. When spaces are smaller, you need to add interest in other ways,' says Jones.

Both bedrooms are light and spacious, partly due to large windows and expansive views. Clear polycarbonate was also used in the pitched roofline to provide additional light in the house.

Edmiston Jones Architects

Photography by Brandt Noack

The Next Phase

After living in an architect-designed house for many years, raising their family, the owners of this new house realised the importance of using an architect. While the new house is considerably smaller, elements such as light were considered crucial. 'There was a preoccupation with light from the start of the design,' says architect Kai Chen, who worked closely with project architect Anne-Marie Treweeke. With this in mind, light, became a driving force in the design of this house.

The house doesn't follow a linear path to the back fence. Instead, it zigzags across the site, framing four courtyards. All the main living spaces have garden views and are filled with light. There is access to the garden from every room, including the main bedroom that is adjacent to the rear garden. 'There's a lack of boundaries. The idea was to keep the spaces as fluid as possible and allow the interior and exterior spaces to blur,' says Chen of Allom Lovell & Associates.

Unlike many smaller spaces, which eliminate corridor spaces wherever possible, in this case, the passages were considered fundamental to the design. Past the front door, there's a corridor to a bedroom and bathroom. Another corridor, at right angles, continues down the other side of the house, past the kitchen, dining room and separate living room. 'Adolf Loos (renowned Viennese architect working in the early part of the 20th century) was known for creating a journey in his homes. There was always a sense of going somewhere,' says Chen. 'The corridor to the second bedroom creates a sense that there's a second wing in the house.'

The kitchen, also accessed from the passage, includes a large sliding door. When the door is left open, the kitchen can borrow additional space from the corridor. 'It's a Japanese practice to borrow space,' says Chen. 'The corridor also doubles as gallery space for the client's paintings,' he adds.

One colour was used for all the walls, a silvery ash colour, tinged with red. 'It's almost volcanic in tone,' says Chen, who used this colour to make connections to the courtyard gardens. As Chen says, 'The corridors in the house are similar to a garden path. If you don't have one, how can you possibly appreciate the garden in its entirety.'

Allom Lovell & Associates   Photography by Peter Bennetts and by Shannon Pawsey

Loft Spaces

This inner-city building was previously used as a silk dying factory. Built in the 1920s, its robust shell was ideal for refurbishment. 'The architectural approach is hard core. The exterior expression of the building reflects its gritty inner-urban location,' says Jones-Evans. The building has a monastic appearance while cleverly disguising a more sensual and interesting spatial composition of industrial spaces within. 'We retained some of the 1920s detailing, such as the art-deco brickwork. But most of the building was gutted,' says architect Dale Jones-Evans, who converted the space to four residential lofts, one commercial loft and five penthouse apartments.

As the building abuts a laneway (and has its own street frontage), Jones-Evans was able to draw on this for additional light. The architects were also able to use the laneway to create separate entrances for each loft. 'We peeled back all the small openings and made massive shopfront openings. They do appear like a retail strip,' says Jones-Evans, who was keen to allow as much light into each loft as possible. 'The occupants are able to pull up a lower blind for privacy. The light can still enter from above,' he adds.

The loft features a large open-plan kitchen, living and dining area on the ground floor, together with a bedroom. On the mezzanine level, there are two additional bedrooms, linked by a bridge, and a bathroom. The ground-floor slab in this loft was removed and replaced at a lower level to allow for the insertion of a mezzanine into the space. The area below, which is used for car parking, featured high ceilings. 'It wasn't necessary to have high ceilings for a car park. We dropped these to the minimum height,' says Jones-Evans.

Instead of walls to segment the spaces, Jones-Evans has used louvred glass walls to define spaces such as the bedrooms. The inner spaces take light and ventilation through these aluminium louvred walls, which are complimented by laminated white glass walls. As Jones-Evans says, 'These walls also act as lanterns of light when they are lit.'

Dale Jones-Evans Pty Ltd   Photography by Trevor Mein and by Dale Jones-Evans

153

A Design Classic

Panoramic views, space and light attracted the owners to buy this apartment in The Domain (formerly known as BP House) Melbourne. Designed in the early 1960s by Demaine Russell Trundle Armstrong & Orton as offices, the space was converted into a three-bedroom apartment in the early 90s. 'Our clients were keen on the views and the space, but they weren't keen on the interior. The planning was quite awkward,' says architect Ilana Kista of Kink Architects, who reworked the apartment with her business partner, architect Nikolas Koulouras.

Designed for a couple whose children had left home, the brief to Kink was to open up the spaces and utilise the view of the parkland opposite. 'They used the words dramatic and theatrical,' says Koulouras. However, instead of reaching for the velvet curtains and thick gold tassels, Kink took a far more glamorous and sophisticated approach. The first thing to be eliminated was the coiffed-ceiling that framed the living area. In its place, a reflective black laminate was used to conceal any beams and staggered edges. Rather than the black ceiling 'shrinking the space', the reflective surface broadens the view and the space, creating a new perspective on the landscape below.

Having one large open space, Kink Architects were also mindful of creating a journey, where everything wasn't instantly apparent from the front door. A large woven mesh stainless-steel curtain creates a veil in the living room. The floor treatments were also relatively undefined. The black granite entrance sporadically edges towards the carpeted living areas. 'We like spaces to overlap. There's a feeling of spaces leaking into each other,' says Koulouras.

While the kitchen is elevated (to conceal the plumbing), the division between the kitchen and dining area is deliberately blurred. 'Our clients were prepared to experiment, but they wanted to be able to see the end result,' says Koulouras. Kink made several models together by generating a number of three-dimensional images on computer. There wouldn't be too many clients who would understand the idea of a carpeted skating ramp leading to the kitchen bench or a unit that swivels out from the kitchen wall to form a breakfast bar against the window. Instead of doors, Kink devised a number of screens. Finished in silver laminate, the screen doors are an art form in themselves.

And while the views, space and light in this apartment continue to impress, it is the renovation that captivates the senses.

This apartment first appeared in Domain, *The Age* newspaper, 15 May 2002.

Kink Architects   Photography by Peter Bennetts

In the Snow

This apartment, one of 25, is located in the snowfields. The development, designed as nine separate buildings, all interconnected by walkways, includes a separate building containing a café and cinema. The project forms part of a small village.

The architects, Provan Burdett, were keen to create something more than concrete-block walled apartments, commonly found in the area. 'We wanted to create a place as enjoyable to stay in as the home they left behind,' says architect David Burdett. As an alternative to many of the concrete rendered apartments, the architects selected a variety of materials: stone, corrugated Colorbond, copper sheeting, corrugated mini-orb and galvanised steel for the balconies. The materials not only break up the scale of the buildings (three and four storey), but also help to create a lighter effect on the ground. 'The mixture creates a visual interest,' adds Burdett.

While one family usually stays in this two-bedroom apartment, on many occasions there are two families. With so many people within the space, one of the most important issues was to create sufficient storage, both for clothing and suitcases for all the cumbersome ski equipment. 'We also had to include a lock-up storage area for the owners of the apartment, who rent it out on a regular basis,' says Burdett.

The apartment, irregular in shape, with angular-shaped balconies, follows the boundaries of the site. 'The site is similar to a hexagon which has been sliced up,' says Burdett. The front door, for example, opens directly into the kitchen/living area. On the first floor is a bedroom and bathroom facilities. And on the mezzanine level there's a second bedroom, complete with its own separate bathroom facilities.

Large stone tiles were used for the kitchen, dining and living area and stainless steel for the kitchen benches. 'The materials had to be robust,' says Burdett, who also ensured double-glazing on all the windows. 'There can be a high amount of traffic in this apartment, not to mention the effect of bringing in and out all the ski equipment.'

Views from the rooftop deck (outside the mezzanine) are memorable, as is the feeling of sitting in the rooftop spa.

Provan Burdett Pty Ltd   Photography by Peter Bennetts

A New Element

This inner-city warehouse was used as an artist's studio for many years. While a studio was still required by the current owner, also an artist, so too was a new home for his family. Rather than looking for separate premises for a studio and house, the two were combined under the one roof.

The new townhouse, which clearly rises from its old warehouse shell, was designed by architect Col Bandy. 'I wanted the design to appear as a confident new object and largely disconnected from the old warehouse,' says Bandy. The new structure emerges through the original building like an oilrig, visible from streets nearby.

The studio was completely retained, with only four new columns, the stairs and the floor providing an additional layer to the home. A primary steel-structure system was used to reinforce the new work. 'The steelwork is extremely light and spans large distances. It's capable of taking substantial loads,' says Bandy, who expressed the steel aesthetic in the design.

The owner's work studio was left intact on the ground level but a new study was inserted into the space, as well as a light court to provide additional light. On the first floor is the kitchen, open-plan living and dining, together with a bedroom and bathroom. On the third level is the main bedroom and a study or alternatively a guest's bedroom. To link the two upper levels, Bandy included a void over the living area (soaring to nearly 6 metres).

While the new work (kitchens, bathrooms and so on) is clearly evident, so are the aged red bricks that line the internal spaces. Splattered paint on the walls framing the new timber staircase is as appreciated as the latest surfaces and finishes used in the project. There is a similar contrast between the thickness of the original walls and the lightness of steel. For the owner, the pleasure of the house is being able to put down his palette and return to work, in his own time.

Col Bandy P/L Architects   Photography by Richard Lenartowicz

New Life for a Terrace

This Victorian terrace has been completely redesigned by architect Stephen Varady. Bought by the current owners in virtually original condition, it presented itself as a series of small, enclosed rooms. 'We retained the original footprint, but it has been completely reworked for contemporary living,' says Varady.

Originally, there was a timber staircase that doglegged its way to the second floor. Varady used the pathway down the side of the terrace and additional exterior space for the new staircase. Enclosed by toughened glass, the staircase now cuts an impressive swathe across the centre of the house. And as there wasn't room for a cellar, Varady punctuated the undercroft of the staircase with circular cavities to store wine.

A new kitchen and family room was added to the terrace, in a strong and contemporary manner. 'We were prepared to retain some of the skirtings and architraves of the original house. But when the new wing started to appear, the owners were keen to go with clean lines throughout the entire house,' says Varady. The strong contemporary lines of the design are echoed in the sculptural black beams that appear throughout the house. 'They tie in the old and the new. They were inspired by Stanley Kubric's film *2001 Space Odyssey*. In the film there were a series of monoliths. You weren't quite sure why they were there,' he says.

While the function of the beams remains unclear, the use of graphic stripes in the renovation is succinct. 'I wanted to make a feature of this wall (which encloses the bathroom and laundry),' says Varady, who used seven different shades of blue and green. 'It's like a piece of art but it also illuminates the more recessed part of the house.' While many think small spaces require small gestures, others such as Varady prefer a few strong and bold statements.

Stephen Varady Architecture   Photography by Stephen Varady

A New Addition

This Victorian terrace was completely reworked by BBP Architects. While the original part of the house (formal front room and upstairs bedroom) were relatively untouched, the house had been added to over the years in a haphazard way.

The front two rooms were retained, together with a bluestone cellar below the house. The later additions were removed and one large open-plan kitchen and living area was created. While the cellar was previously concealed, it is now accessible via a perforated steel balustrade framing the original bluestone steps. The new kitchen is relatively open to the living area and is defined by a central island bench. To maximise space in the kitchen, the fridge, pantry and storage areas are tucked into the staircase leading to the floor above.

While there is a clear division between the old and the new, BBP architects retained the generous ceiling heights in the new wing (approximately 3.5 metres). However, what makes the spaces feel considerably larger is the use of skylights in the house, one over the kitchen area and one above the staircase leading to the cellar. There's also an elliptical-shaped skylight over the living area. 'The width of the rooms is only about 5 metres so it was important to bring as much light as possible into the interior to create the sense of space,' says architect David Balestra-Pimpini.

Upstairs, a second bedroom was also added. Made of corrugated steel, the new bedroom/study was designed at an angle to the rectilinear form of the original Victorian terrace. The change of form not only defines the new work, but also allowed for skylights to be inserted into the deck on the first floor. 'The angle of the new room prevents overlooking from neighbouring homes,' adds Balestra-Pimpini.

BBP Architects   Photography by Chris Ott

PORCH

LOUNGE

POWDER ROOM

L'DRY.

KITCHEN

DINING

LOUNGE

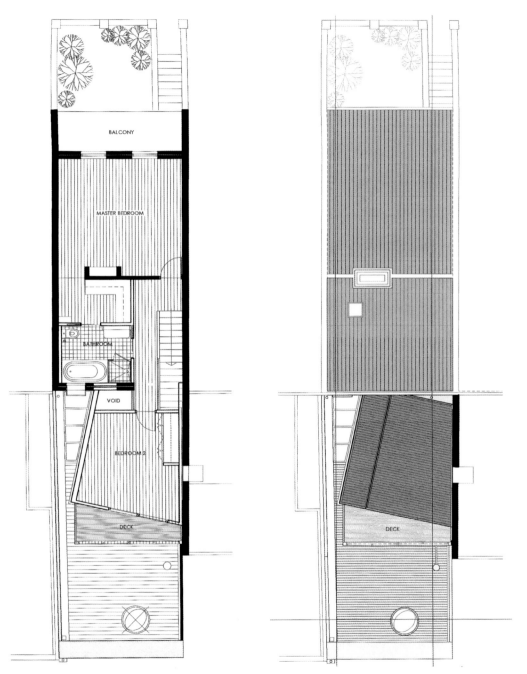

BALCONY

MASTER BEDROOM

BATHROOM

VOID

BEDROOM 2

DECK

DECK

A Warehouse

This warehouse, built in a back lane in the late 1800s, was originally a stable. 'It had a hip tin roof and the walls were about to collapse. It was close to derelict,' says architect Michael Rahill.

While the walls were in a precarious state, the architect and owners found the distressed brickwork appealing. Instead of pulling the 100-square-metre building down and building new walls, a new inner wall was applied. 'It now has strength, while still retaining that grungy feel to the lane,' says Rahill.

The brief from the owners was to divide the space in two to accommodate their professional work. One side would operate as a photography studio, the other side as an artist's studio. In complete contrast to one another, the photographer's studio is painted black, the artist's studio, white. 'The photographer needs to control the light (artificial), so the brief excluded windows,' says Rahill, who created a new skylight in the artist's studio. There is a strong play of light and shadow in this home. As Rahill says, 'It was an exercise in borrowing light and using skylights to draw in light from above.'

The space is divided by a central unit, which comprises a darkroom (completely enclosed), an open galley-style kitchen and an enclosed bathroom. Simply constructed in plaster and studwork, the white walls reflect the sunlight into the artist's studio, which includes space for a bed. Even though there are also no windows in the artist's studio, there are floor-to-ceiling glass doors to a courtyard garden.

Original Oregon trusses were also retained. The old timber trusses are clearly differentiated by splattered paint. 'Alone they weren't strong enough to support the roof. To comply with current building regulations, we had to add new trusses,' says Rahill, who used rough sawn pine to line the ceiling. 'It gives it that rustic look,' he adds.

Michael Rahill Architect   Photography by Robert Colvin

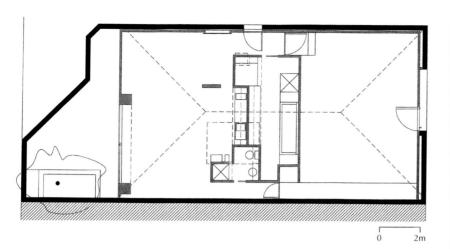

Irregular Shapes

This property originally consisted of a large double-storey terrace house facing a busy thoroughfare and a small garage facing a quiet side street. When the owners bought the property, it was the garage they were interested in living in, rather than the large house. 'The plan was to renovate the terrace and turn the garage into an apartment-style home,' says architect Craig Rossetti.

Built in the 1960s, the garage is nestled into an irregular-shaped site. Typical of many inner-city sites, there is a shortage of off-street car parking. Rossetti was not only asked to provide car parking for the apartment, but also to include parking for the adjoining terrace. After providing car spaces for the two dwellings, there was still sufficient room for a study/second bedroom, a bathroom and laundry facilities on the ground floor. 'Our planning applications were submitted in the form of 1:50 (normally 1:100). Everything was tight. There was concern we wouldn't be able to get the stairs in,' says Rossetti.

The 70-square-metre home (excluding car parking) features a generous open-plan kitchen, dining and living area on the first floor. This level also includes the main bedroom and ensuite facilities. While the dimensions of the spaces are small, there's a sense of spaciousness. 'It doesn't feel confined. All the internal angles (as a result of the shape of the site) energise the space and make you think that there's always something beyond,' says Maggie Jory who lives in the house.

Rossetti also extended the space by incorporating a narrow external balcony. The 1-metre-width balcony is framed with a bamboo screen. 'There's a sense of the outdoors. You can look over the bamboo towards the church spires. The light can also filter through the bamboo into the interior,' says Rossetti.

A cut-out window at the top of the staircase allows the space to be appreciated even while mounting the stairs, and at every turn, there's a window to look out of. As Rossetti says, 'It's about working with circulation patterns. Where are people going to walk? And where is the furniture going to be placed? You need to really think about these things from the start. There just isn't any room for mistakes.'

Craig Rossetti Architect   Photography by Andrew Ashton

A School

This loft-style apartment was previously part of a school. One of 10 lofts constructed within the 1920s building, the architect was keen to create a feeling of space. Rather than conceal the building's origins, the structural bays, columns and beams are given their full expression. Even the height of the space (5.2 metres) is maintained throughout the loft.

The loft is accessed from a steel mesh chassis, which has been clipped to the side of the building and contains walkways, stairs and terraces. Inside the loft, the space is designed to be flexible. On the first floor there is a kitchen, bathroom and laundry, together with a living area. And tucked into a corner is a study that can be screened off should privacy be required.

On the mezzanine above are the main bedroom, ensuite bathroom and a studio that appears to cantilever over the dramatic void. With its partly steel mesh floor and open steel balustrade, the studio seems to float effortlessly in the space. The loft was designed for living and working, and, as the mezzanine studio is generous in length, it allows for up to three workstations. 'If you need an extra bedroom, the small study on the ground level can be converted,' says architect Dale Jones-Evans. A timber screen is currently used to define this space.

The main bedroom upstairs, framed by louvred glass walls, also blurs the division between the spaces. The louvred walls not only create additional light in the bedroom but also allow for cross-ventilation in the loft. Rather than try and conceal the building's structure, the architect has finely woven the new work into the original structure. The glass louvres framing the main bedroom have been carefully designed around the beam.

As Jones-Evans says, 'We simply repolished and lined the original floorboards and the walls are raw plaster. It was important to retain the industrial language of the interior.'

Dale Jones-Evans Pty Ltd   Photography by Chris Cole and by Dale Jones-Evans

An Abstraction of the Landscape

These two inner-city townhouses were built on a compact site. Measuring 11 by 14 metres, the only outdoor space that could be provided was for car parking. To create a sense of landscape in this fairly industrial environment, the architects brought colour into the design.

'There was a creeper on a neighbouring wall. It was the only greenery in the area,' says architect Graham Burrows of Jackson Clements Burrows Architects. 'The two shades of green (used on the exterior as well as in the interior) are similar to the light and shade of a leaf,' he adds. While the townhouses do not have a leafy aspect, there is a strong connection with the outdoors. 'The idea was like a tree that had grown into the building,' says Burrows who also used two tones of green to line the balustrade for the upstairs landing.

The townhouse (featured) is approximately 95 square metres in size. On the ground floor are a car space, two bedrooms and a bathroom. On the first floor is the kitchen, dining and living area, which opens to a small deck area. 'It was a fairly tight site so we had to work to the extremities of the site,' says Burrows.

Jackson Clements Burrows designed the living area on the top floor to take advantage of the light. The architects also wanted to make the second level feel as generous as possible. As a result, the ceiling height on the second level starts at 2.7 metres and extends to 4 metres (adjacent to the balcony). Large bi-fold glass doors (also 2.7 metres in height) are complimented with celestial glass louvred windows. And as protection from the harsher light, the architects extended the roof to form a canopy over the deck.

While the open-plan living area is generous, the architects enhanced the feeling of space by using Blackbutt timber on the floors and extending this material to the outdoor deck and balustrade. 'There's a sense that the space is drawn out before it is folded back up,' says Burrows. 'We wanted to create a feeling of going beyond four walls,' he adds.

The floor-to-ceiling windows in the living area also help to extend the space. The architects used polycarbonate sheeting in some of the windows and even for the overhead skylights. 'They look like bands of light moving across the space rather than fixed windows.'

The two townhouses appear like one house from the street. The building's solid rendered plinth extends to the street's edge. And metal cladding used for the roof and upper walls creates a lighter contrast.

Jackson Clements Burrows Pty Ltd Architects

Photography by Shannon Mcgrath

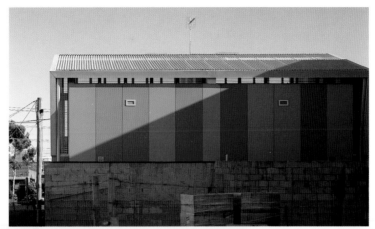

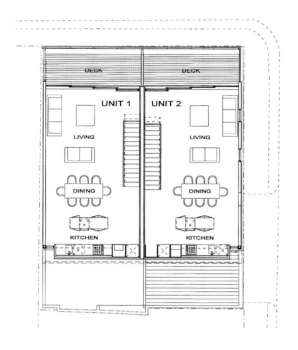

184

Utilising the Space

Located on a small inner-city site, measuring only 5 by 20 metres, one of the main issues when building this home was privacy. The two neighbouring houses, both double-storey, overlooked the site. 'Everyone in the area is keen to include a second storey. The city views from this location are extensive,' says architect Jude Doyle.

The new two-storey masonry, glass and steel house occupies 75 per cent of the site. On the ground floor is the studio and washing-up area, designed for the owner who is a potter (there's also a kiln in the corner of the backyard). Upstairs, are the living, kitchen and bathroom, together with the main bedroom and a small Juliet-style balcony. To create privacy in the bedroom, Doyle fitted the window with a floor-to-ceiling timber-slatted screen.

The two levels of the house are connected by a steel staircase with perforated steel treads. The staircase not only adds an industrial aesthetic to the home, but also allows light to filter between the two levels. 'The materials are reasonably light. It's a narrow space and I didn't want to use anything that appeared too heavy,' says Doyle.

As the spaces are small, Doyle had in the back of her mind the type of furniture that would be appropriate. Small module-style furniture and narrow elongated tables were used to free up as much floor space as possible.

While the present arrangement suits the current owner, the spaces were designed to be flexible. The studio for example, could be used as a second bedroom. Alternatively, the ground-floor space could double as a second more informal living area. As Doyle says, 'Small spaces require you to be inventive. The constraints can act as a positive.'

Doyle Architect Pty Ltd   Photography by Derek Swalwell

End to End

On a corner site, the front townhouse faces the street, the other, a narrow laneway behind. 'Our client wanted two small units, one she could live in with her son, the other to rent out,' says architect Nic Bochsler.

Surrounded by single-storey Victorian-style homes, there was a conscious decision to reduce the scale of the new townhouses. Bochsler used bricks for the ground floor and predominantly glass for the second storey. To reduce the scale even further, horizontal aluminium louvres were used to frame the upper level. 'They create a sense of privacy, filter the light and draw the eye to street level,' says Bochsler.

On the ground floor are two bedrooms, ensuites and laundry facilities, together with off-street car parking. On the first floor, there is one continuous space, articulated by a bulkhead. 'We used the bulkhead to conceal the air-conditioning unit, along with some of the other services. It also helps define the three living areas (kitchen, dining and living),' says Bochsler. The bookshelf between the dining area and the lounge helps to enclose the spaces. 'You can see through the entire space, but not from every angle,' he adds.

While the spaces are fairly generous, Bochsler was keen to maximise the sense of space. The timber floorboards, for example, have been stained black, along with the timber deck adjacent to the living area. In the entrance, the lower portion of the staircase has been opened up to the passage. As Bochsler says, 'The townhouses have a slight warehouse feel. From the outside it appears quite enclosed. But when you reach the second level it completely opens out.'

Bochsler & Partners   Photography by Neil Lorimer

Making Space Work

Originally there were two houses on this site, one facing the main street, the other facing the laneway at the rear. But when the architect/owners bought the site, the rear cottage had already been removed. 'We decided to renovate the front house and build a new house at the rear for us to live in,' says architect Abbie Galvin who designed the house with her partner David Astridge.

As the development site is only 5 by 13 metres, the architects made every centimetre count. The sidewalls are exposed concrete block. 'We love the rawness of the material. It also increased the sense of space by not adding another layer such as plaster,' says Galvin. The front and back walls are either glass or yellow cedar. 'The cedar will fade to a silvery grey,' she adds. The translucent glass wall benefits from a large Jacaranda tree in the street. The morning sunlight casts a silhouette of the tree on the glass.

The house is approximately 80 square metres in size. There is a combined living and dining area on the ground floor that opens directly to a garden through full-length bi-fold glass doors. The kitchen, which runs along one side of the house, conceals the service areas such as the laundry. The kitchen joinery, which is made of a honed black granite benchtop and black polyurethane cupboards, appears to recede from the living area. 'It's like a piece of furniture,' says Galvin. And to maximise the space, part of the steel-tread staircase hovers over the kitchen bench.

The bedrooms upstairs were designed to be flexible. Originally designed as a house without children, a wardrobe unit was inserted into the upstairs space to provide two separate rooms a few years later. 'It's a freestanding robe, with storage on either side. It can easily be moved around to create two bedrooms of the same size. Alternatively the space can be reconfigured into a larger bedroom and a smaller study. It can also be placed up against one wall,' says Galvin.

The house feels considerably more spacious that its actual size. As Galvin says, 'When you are working with small spaces, you need to think about circulation. Where the furniture should go can't be an afterthought.'

Astridge Galvin Architects   Photography by Brett Boardman

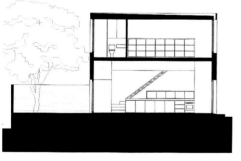

Architects

Allom Lovell & Associates
35 Little Bourke Street
Melbourne, Victoria 3000
Ph: +(61) 3 9662 3344
Fax: +(61) 3 9662 1037
Email: ala@allom-lovell.com.au
Page 146

Alsocan Architects
455 Swan Street
Richmond, Victoria 3121
Ph: +(61) 3 9421 3433
Fax: +(61) 3 9421 3422
Email: alsocan@alphalink.com.au
Page 140

Architects Johannsen + Associates Pty Ltd
2 Liverpool Lane
East Sydney, NSW 2010
Ph: +(61) 2 9360 9833
Fax: +(61) 2 9360 9101
Email: mail@aja.com.au
Page 88

Astridge Galvin Architects
David Astridge + Abbie Galvin
72 Great Buckingham Street
Redfern, NSW 2016
Ph/Fax: +(61) 2 9319 7754
Page 192

Baenziger Coles Architects
419 City Road
South Melbourne, Victoria 3205
Ph: +(61) 3 9696 6899
Fax: +(61) 3 9696 1958
Email: mail@baenzigercoles.com.au
Page 62

BBP Architects
93 Kerr Street
Fitzroy, Victoria 3065
Ph: +(61) 3 9416 1486
Fax: +(61) 3 9416 1438
Email: info@bbparchitects.com
Page 170

Black Kosloff Knott Pty Ltd
Level 9, 180 Russell Street
Melbourne, Victoria 3000
Ph: +(61) 3 9671 4555
Fax: +(61) 3 9671 4666
Email: black@b-k-k.com.au
Page 132

Bochsler & Partners
5 Edward Street
Toorak, Victoria 3142
Ph: +(61) 3 9827 2988
Fax: +(61) 3 9827 2722
Email: bochsler@bochsler.com
Page 188

Brearley Architects and Urban Designers
Level 2, 358 Lonsdale Street
Melbourne, Victoria 3000
Ph: +(61) 3 9642 5115
Fax: +(61) 3 9642 5114
Email: archi@bau.com.au
Page 60

Burne Hocking Weimar Architects
Level 6, 258 Little Bourke Street
Melbourne, Victoria 3000
Ph: +(61) 3 9663 3950
Fax: +(61) 3 9662 9710
Email: AIABHW@bigpond.com.au
Page 28

Chenchow Little Architects
422 Bourke Street
Surry Hills, NSW 2010
Ph: +(61) 2 9357 4333
Fax: +(61) 2 9357 4334
Email: tony@chenchowlittle.com
Page 106

Col Bandy P/L Architects
4 Upton Road
Windsor, Victoria 3182
Ph: +(61) 3 9529 8722
Fax: +(61) 3 9529 7917
Email: colbandy@mira.net
Page 162

Coy & Yiontis Architects
Level 2/387 Clarendon Street
South Melbourne, Victoria 3205
Ph: +(61) 3 9645 7600
Fax: +(61) 3 9645 7622
Email: cy@cyarchitects.com.au
Page 96

Craig Rossetti Architect
28 Gwynne Street
Richmond, Victoria 3121
Ph: +(61) 3 9428 4812
Fax: +(61) 3 9421 1110
Email: craig@rossetti.com.au
Page 176

Dale Jones-Evans Pty Ltd
Loft 1, 50–54 Ann Street
Surry Hills, NSW 2010
Ph: +(61) 2 9211 0626
Fax: +(61) 2 9211 5998
Email: dje@dje.com.au
Pages 152 and 180

David Hicks Pty Ltd Design
302/11 Hillingdon Place
Prahran, Victoria 3181
Ph: +(61) 3 9525 0331
Fax: +(61) 3 9525 0395
Email: davidhicksdesign@aol.com
Page 44

David Luck Architecture
17 Hardy Street
South Yarra, Victoria 3141
Ph/Fax: +(61) 3 9867 7509
Email: david.luck@bigpond.com.au
Page 126

David Neil Architects
203 Canterbury Road
Canterbury, Victoria 3126
Ph: +(61) 3 9836 5300
Fax: +(61) 3 9836 5400
Email: davidneilarchitect@primus.com.au
Page 78

Dawson Brown Architecture
Level 1/63 William Street
East Sydney, NSW 2010
Ph: +(61) 2 9360 7977
Fax: +(61) 2 9360 2123
Email: dba@carolinecasey.com.au
Page 98

Des Holmes Architects Pty Ltd
Suite 6, 37–43 Bridge Road
Richmond, Victoria 3121
Ph: +(61) 3 9428 3834
Fax: +(61) 3 9428 5911
Email: dholmes@corplink.com.au
Page 36

Doyle Architect Pty Ltd
318 Clarke Street
Northcote, Victoria 3070
Ph: +(61) 3 9486 7586
Fax: +(61) 3 9489 4826
Email: jood@hotkey.net.au
Page 186

Edmiston Jones Architects
49 Bridge Road
Nowra, NSW 2541
Ph: +(61) 2 4421 6822
Fax: +(61) 2 4422 1963
Email: aej@aej.com.au
Page 144

Grant Amon Architect
Room 102/125 Fitzroy Street
St. Kilda, Victoria 3182
Ph: +(61) 3 9593 9944
Fax: +(61) 3 9593 9697
Email: gamon@smart.net.au
Page 22

Holan Joubert Architects
202 Little Page Street
Middle Park, Victoria 3206
Ph: +(61) 3 9696 8140
Fax: +(61) 3 9696 8005
Email: hjarc@optusnet.com.au
Page 102

Inarc Architects Pty Ltd
22 Liddiard Street
Hawthorn, Victoria 3122
Ph: +(61) 3 9819 0677
Fax: +(61) 3 9819 0244
Email: info@inarc.com.au
Page 12

Jackson Clements Burrows Pty Ltd Architects
One Harwood Place
Melbourne, Victoria 3000
Ph: +(61) 3 9654 6227
Fax: +(61) 3 9654 6195
Email: jacksonclementsburrows@jcba.com.au
Page 182

Jan + Manton Design Architecture
11 Amsterdam Street
Richmond, Victoria 3121
Ph: +(61) 3 9429 7744
Fax: +(61) 3 9429 3955
Email: jm@janmanton.com.au
Page 38

Kennedy Nolan Architects
195a Brunswick Street
Fitzroy, Victoria 3065
Ph: +(61) 3 9415 8971
Fax: +(61) 3 9415 8973
Email: email@kennedynolan.com.au
Page 54

Kink Architects
Level 3, 17–19 Elizabeth Street
Melbourne, Victoria 3000
Ph: +(61) 3 9629 9992
Email: ilana@kink.com.au
Page 154

Lacoste + Stevenson Architects
85 William Street
East Sydney, NSW 2011
Ph: +(61) 2 9360 8633
Fax: +(61) 2 9380 6231
Email: lacoste@cyber.net.au
Page 92

Lahz Nimmo Architects Pty Ltd
Level 5, 116–122 Kippax Street
Surry Hills, NSW 2010
Ph: +(61) 2 9211 1220
Fax: +(61) 2 9211 1554
Email: annabel@lahznimmo.com
Page 122

Marcus O'Reilly Architect
70A Chatsworth Road
Prahran, Victoria 3181
Ph: +(61) 3 9510 6023
Fax: +(61) 3 9510 6053
Email: marcus@marcusoreilly.com
Page 56

Melocco & Moore Architects Pty Ltd
Level 5, 122 Kippax Street
Surry Hills, NSW 2010
Ph: +(61) 2 9212 6111
Fax: +(61) 2 9212 2050
Email: architects@meloccomoore.com.au
Page 68

Michael Rahill Architect
289 Flinders Lane
Melbourne, Victoria 3000
Ph: +(61) 3 9639 5838
Fax: +(61) 3 9650 0308
Email: michael@rahill.net
Page 48 and 174

Neil + Idle Architects Pty Ltd
21 Balmain Street
Richmond, Victoria 3121
Ph: +(61) 3 9428 5600
Fax: +(61) 3 9428 9001
Email: info@neil-idle.com.au
Page 20

Neometro Architects
Studio 4/15 Inkerman Street
St. Kilda, Victoria 3182
Ph: +(61) 3 9534 7774
Fax: +(61) 3 9534 4644
Email: neometro@neometro.com.au
Pages 42 and 50

O'Connor + Houle Architecture
70 Dow Street
South Melbourne, Victoria 3205
Ph: +(61) 3 9686 7022
Fax: +(61) 3 9686 7033
Email: beebee@ozonline.com.au
Page 72

Provan Burdett Pty Ltd
22 Franklin Place
West Melbourne, Victoria 3003
Ph: +(61) 3 9329 3443
Fax: +(61) 3 9329 3445
Emaill: architects@provanburdett.com.au
Pages 16 and 158

Richard Swansson Architect
118 Brighton Road
Elsternwick, Victoria 3185
Ph: +(61) 3 9531 3290
Fax: +(61) 3 9537 7740
Page 128

Shania Shegedyn Photographers
11 Anderson Street
West Melbourne, Victoria 3000
Ph: +(61) 411 029 939
Email: shaniatom@optusnet.com.au
Page 66

SJB Architects
25 Coventry Street
Southbank, Victoria 3006
Ph: +(61) 3 9699 6688
Fax: +(61) 3 9696 6234
Email: arch@sjb.com.au
Page 116

Stanic Harding Pty Ltd
123 Commonwealth Street
Surry Hills, NSW 2010
Ph: +(61) 2 9211 6710
Fax: +(61) 2 9211 0366
Email: architects@stanicharding.com.au
Page 134

Stephen Jolson Architect
Studio 1/251 Chapel Street
Prahran, Victoria 3181
Ph: +(61) 3 9533 7997
Fax: +(61) 3 9533 7978
Email: stephen@sjarchitect.com
Page 108

Stephen Varady Architecture
14 Lackey Street
St. Peters, NSW 2044
Ph: +(61) 2 9516 4044
Fax: +(61) 2 9516 4541
Email: svarady@bigpond.com.au
Pages 76 and 164

Studio 101 Architects
101 Kilgour Street
Geelong, Victoria 3220
Ph: +(61) 3 5221 9131
Fax: +(61) 3 5221 0831
Email: woolard@studio101.com.au
Page 30

Swaney Draper Pty Ltd Architects
376 Albert Street
East Melbourne, Victoria 3002
Ph: +(61) 3 9417 6162
Fax: +(61) 3 9419 4480
Email: mail@swaneydraper.com.au
Page 112

Utz-Sanby Architects
Level 1, 4 Young Street
Neutral Bay, NSW 2089
Ph: + (61) 2 9904 2515
Fax: + (61) 2 9904 2626
Email: utzsanby@idx.com.au
Page 82

Acknowledgments

I would like to thank all the architects featured in this book. While the projects they designed are relatively small in scale, the ideas and level of creativity are immeasurably larger. I would also like to thank the many photographers who contributed to making this book appear much larger and more impressive. I would especially like to thank my partner, Naomi Crafti, for her support.

Some of the work in this book has appeared in *The Age* newspaper as listed below.

Page 22: 'A Georgian Townhouse' by Grant Amon Architect, photography by Earl Carter and by Richard Briglia. This house first appeared in Domain, *The Age* newspaper, 25 June 2003.

Page 30: 'Maximising the Site' by Studio 101 Architects, photography by Trevor Mein. This house first appeared in Domain, *The Age* newspaper, 16 October 2002.

Page 54: 'External Rooms' by Kennedy Nolan Architects, photography by Derek Swalwell. This house first appeared in Domain, *The Age* newspaper, 5 June 2002.

Page 154: 'A Design Classic' by Kink Architects, photography by Peter Bennetts. This apartment first appeared in Domain, *The Age* newspaper, 15 May 2002.

The following project first appeared in Australian *Vogue Living* magazine, April/May issue, 2000:
'A Small Gem' by O'Connor + Houle Architecture, photography by Peter Clarke.

Every effort has been made to trace the original source of copyright material contained in this book. The publishers would be pleased to hear from copyright holders to rectify any errors or omissions. The information and illustrations in this publication have been prepared and supplied by the entrants. While all reasonable efforts have been made to source the required information and ensure accuracy, the publishers do not, under any circumstances, accept responsibility for errors, omissions and representations expressed or implied.

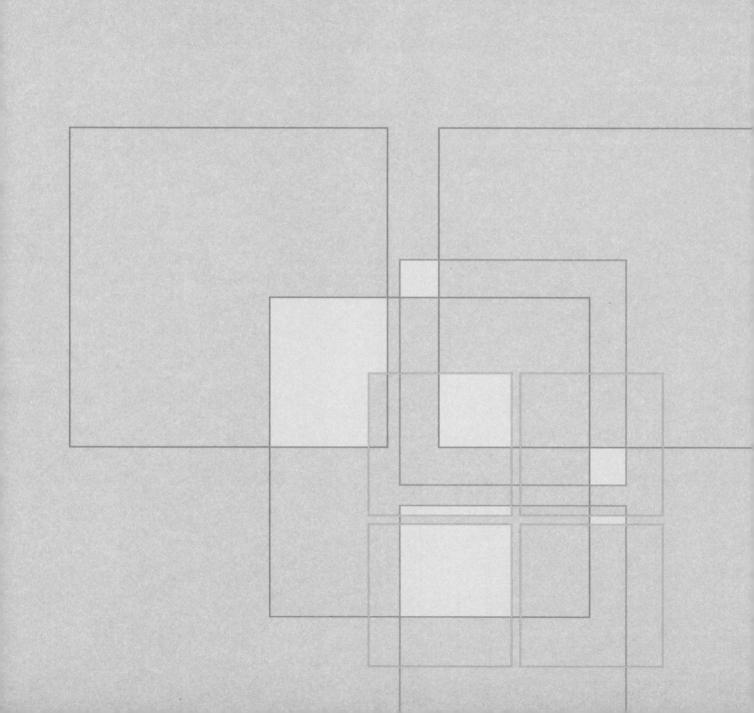